"After reading this b
shall all men know th
another' John 13:35. .... with
practical strategies and biblical accuracy in the breakthrough message
of *Belong*. It's the remedy that will restore vital unity, enabling us to
relate to one another as believers who belong not only to Christ but to
one another in the Body of Christ. Because Toni and Rachel have lived
this out both in their personal mentoring relationship and in their local
church, *Belong* is full of powerful wisdom the reader can grab hold of,
and be set free from the fear of belonging to a local church. This book
is not theory - it is the heart of our Father God for His Bride, His
Children, His Family, and His Church."

— **Dan Chesney**
Senior Pastor
London Alive Church, London UK

"Rachel and Toni have constructed a functional framework—blueprint for life—to develop a fruitful and fulfilling family life. It is my pleasure to affirm both of them as faithful, proven stewards of God's word, servants of the family of God, and sensitive to both the complications and challenges of growing and raising a spiritual family amid the confusion and societal complexities and spiritual issues of the present hour. Without hesitation, I urge the reading, application and proliferation of this resource.

They, along with Pastor Dale Evrist, have a proven stance and stability as spiritual leaders who have long been established through their vitality in the word of God and His Son. Their spiritual discernment and awareness of the transient winds of change (navigated and living it—pastoring in the Nashville environment—obviously—ever-sensitive to the contemporary culture in its nuances) has been essential in perceiving the times.
Like the sons of Issachar...men that had knowledge of the times and what it was best for Israel to do... I Chronicles 12:32."

— **Jack W. Hayford**
Chancellor
The King's University, Southlake, Texas

"*Belong* is a book filled with deep, impacting spiritual truth. It is about belonging, growing, participating, becoming, being welcomed, valued, and accepted as God's chosen daughter or son in His spiritual family—

His Church. It's a book of real-life stories and experiences of being spiritual moms and dads and helping to be spiritual parents to others. There are no perfect parents or families and as a result the images of what family or parenting looks like can be terribly flawed and marred. *Belong*, is both spiritual and very practical in helping to bring a deeper understanding of God's design for how He works to bring hope and healing to many through His Church. Toni and Rachel's life stories are reflected throughout the pages that follow. You will be carried along by their life experiences, as well as helpful insights and practical tools of encouragement. I truly believe this book brings an important, timely word for the Body of Christ and if embraced, the ensuing results—life-changing!"

– Dr. Robb J. Hattem
Associate Pastor
New Life Community Church, Oxnard, CA.

"'What if we aren't living in the fullness of what God has available for us because we simply don't understand?' In *Belong*, Toni Kline and Rachel Cordero respond beautifully to this large question with insight, scriptural principles, and hope shaped by experiencing true spiritual family. They share their journey as friends, sisters in the Lord, teachers and students. Their lives make the case for the priceless value of a healthy spiritual family as God's instrument for wholeness in the body of Christ. Everyone longs to be known deeply yet loved unconditionally. Rachael and Toni testify that this isn't some impossible dream. It is God's desire and design for every believer in Jesus."

– David Shibley
Founder and World Representative
Global Advance

"I love the message of *Belong*! As I read it I felt like our Church family values and dynamics were unfolding before me in the written word. So many treasured faces and pictures were playing in my mind as I read thru the pages of this book. And I was filled with hope for the future of the Church. *Belong*, not only captures so much of our family values, but most of all it glorifies our Heavenly Father and His divine plan for us as His body and His bride! I love these two women and I love being a part of the Father's spiritual family with them.

I pray that as you read the pages of this book you will be freshly filled with hope and with a greater love and commitment to Christ's body—His beautiful Church. A Spiritual Family is available for all of us who make Jesus our Love, passion and mission. As you embrace the message of *Belong*, you too will experience real health and wholeness so that you can fully be the person that God created you to be!"

– **Joan Evrist**
Associate Pastor and Lead Evangelist
New Song Christian Fellowship, Brentwood TN

"One of the greatest needs in our cities today is for godly, mature men to father, lead, mentor, inspire, love, care for and pray for the next generation who has been abandoned, overlooked, or orphaned by their natural fathers. My wife, Carol, and I are honored to serve as spiritual parents and mentors for many young people. Take it from us, breaking open your hearts, doors and calendars to these children of God is a worthwhile sacrifice that restores culture and redeems precious lives. This book helps to reshape the modern church's selfish and narrow definition of "family" into one that Jesus modeled."

– **Mark H. Maxwell**
Entertainment Attorney
Belmont University Adjunct Professor

"*Belong* is a book filled with the testimony of two people who show that healing and health come by being deeply rooted in a spiritual community. In an age when many people who claim to be Christians only "attend" church and dabble with the spiritual family, the Bible calls us to growth and live life fully integrated with one another. Toni and Rachel, while having different life experiences, prove the point that we desperately need the power of God and the presence of one another to fulfill all He has for us. I do not know two people who emulate the message in this book better than they do. I am thankful they have brought this truth to bear in writing as it is so evident in their lives."

– **Scott Weaver**
Executive Pastor
New Song Christian Fellowship, Brentwood TN

"A healthy family doesn't just happen. Rachel Cordero and Toni Kline paint a bigger picture of what family looks like and a step-by-step approach to redeem the past and create a spiritual family of authenticity and love."

– Brian Glassford
Producer, Emergent Productions
Communications Pastor, The Church at Rocky Peak

Christianity is all about family. When we give our lives to Jesus we are restored to right relationship with God as our Father and fellow Christians as brothers and sisters. *Belong* not only shares this reality but imparts a vision of what this could and should be for the body of Christ. This book was clear and compelling as the authors bring you through their journey and Scriptural study of what the Church is truly called to be, what Jesus paid for us to be; a family. As you read this book let the principles sink into your heart and draw you toward the richness of spiritual family that all of us truly long for in Christ.

– Benjamin Dixon
Director of Ignite Global Ministries
Author of "Hearing God"

Since 1999 my wife and I have lived in South Asia parenting children who were formerly orphaned, trafficked, or abandoned. Whether God is calling you to mentor the next generation — or you ARE the next generation — I believe you will find this book to be a biblical and quintessential guide for your journey.

–Dan Ingle
Follower of Jesus, Husband, Dad and Pastor
Studio Ten Ministries | Guardian Village

Belong

Understanding God's Heart for Spiritual Family

Rachel Cordero & Toni Kline

Belong – Understanding God's Heart for Spiritual Family

Copyright © 2016 Rachel Cordero & Toni Kline

All rights reserved. No portion of this book may be reproduced, stored in a retrieval system, or transmitted in any form or by any means—electronic, mechanical, photocopy, recording, scanning, or other—except for brief quotations, without the prior written permission of the publisher.

Published in Nashville, Tennessee, by Crowned Image Publishing.

www.crownedimage.com

Special discounts are available on quantity purchases by corporations, associations, and others. Orders by US trade bookstores and wholesalers—for details, contact the publisher at the website above.

Unless otherwise indicated, all Scripture quotations are taken from The New King James Version (NKJV), copyright © 1979, 1980, 1982, Thomas Nelson, Inc. Used by permission. All rights reserved.

Editors: Helga Geeslin, Kaniel Geeslin, Danielle Caveny
Authors' Photo: Amy Conner

Printed in the United States of America

First Edition, 2016
ISBN:978-0692629932

Dedication

We would like to dedicate this book to two incredible pastoral couples who have made a tremendous impact in both of our lives.

To Dr. Howard and Lolie Wright.

Mom and Dad/Nana and Granddad, you have been a beautiful example of loving Christian parents as well as faithful pastors. You both sacrificially model the selflessness and love of Jesus. It is breathtaking the way you have opened your hearts and your home to many spiritual children, grandchildren and now great-grandchildren. We love you more than words can say, and we are deeply grateful for the gift of you in our lives.

To Pastors Dale and Joan Evrist.

You came to Nashville over 20 years ago with a vision in your hearts from the Lord and a deep love for, and commitment to, His people. More lives have been impacted and changed because of your ministry than one could possibly count. You both consistently model the value and necessity of living in community—especially understanding and embracing spiritual family. You have been faithful and unrelenting in the pursuit of the church as a family. You are devoted, steadfast, and honorable spiritual parents. Thank you for imparting to us the importance of raising up spiritual sons and daughters! This book would not have been written apart from your personal sacrifice of discipling, mentoring and coaching spiritual brothers, sisters, sons and daughters. You have had an eternal impact on both of us! We are humbled and grateful, and we love you very much.

Contents

Foreword
Introduction

One	Perspective	1
Two	What is Family?	17
Three	Why Do I Need Another Family?	25
Four	God, Family & Me	39
Five	Calling All Spiritual Parents!	51
Six	Calling All Spiritual Kids!	69
Seven	Who Asks Whom to Dance? Practical Steps for Relating	87
Eight	Beware, It's Messy! Part 1 The Granddaddy of Them All	103
Nine	Beware, It's Messy! Part 2 Other Tricky Little Boogers	117
Ten	Truly Fruitful	131

Testimonies
About the Authors

Foreword
by Pastor Dale Evrist

When my wife, Joan, and I moved to Nashville, Tennessee to follow a God-given dream in our hearts to plant a new church, we had something very specific in mind. We wanted to birth a spiritual family that loved God and one another deeply from the heart. A family that would be a safe and dynamic environment where holistic help would be offered and holistic healing would be realized. A people that would come to understand church as it is fundamentally revealed in the Scriptures: a covenantal community of brothers and sisters, sons and daughters and mothers and fathers in the Lord.

Most people are looking for a place and a people where and to whom they belong. Individuals, created in the image of God, instinctively look for a context and a community where they will be acknowledged and accepted, embraced and enjoyed. They look for it in relatives, church attendance, neighborhoods, social and service clubs, sports teams, gyms, the corner bar, etc. As much as all of this offers some level of community-belonging, the book you're holding in your hand will propose the notion that the holiest and healthiest place to belong is the family of God, and that it is God Himself who "sets the solitary in families" (Psalm 68:6). And that finding your fit in God's family will provide something deeper, more purposeful and more spiritually and emotionally satisfying than you would find any other place.

Let me hasten to say here that they and I strongly believe in biological families. We have always sought to strengthen and not separate families. Strong marriages and families are at the core of what makes any society strong and stable. The church, locally and globally is in fact a "family of families." But as we all know, not everyone was raised in an environment of spiritual health and emotional wholeness. And some were, in fact, raised in environments that were toxic and abusive. Whatever the case, God the Father in His infinite grace and wisdom, worked through the death of His Son the means by which we could be joined to Himself, our Lord and King Jesus, and to one another in loving bonds of vital love and life in the word and the Spirit. Rachel Cordero and Toni Kline, the authors of this book, will explain to you how the power of spiritual family has greatly enhanced what has been good in their lives and graciously freed them from what has not been good. And in telling their story, they will instruct you in how to experience the same kind of love and liberty in your own life.

You are going to enjoy Rachel and Toni. They have deeply engaged their subject and deeply embraced its substance. This is their story and testimony of how the impact of spiritual family has dramatically shaped and transformed their lives. To me personally, they are two beloved sisters in Christ and two beloved spiritual daughters as well. They are biblically balanced on this topic, looking to help people develop warm, genuine familial relationships in the Spirit, without any trappings of unbiblical desires to cajole or control others. Rachel and Toni believe in "covering, not smothering" and "counsel, not control." You are in good hands with these competent women who have walked this path together as a spiritual mother and daughter, devoted wives, as well as spiritual leaders in Jesus' church and God's family for many years.

As you pick up Belong, You will be welcomed through an open door into a warm place where you will be loved, celebrated, instructed, corrected and cared for—welcomed into the possibility and promise of healthy spiritual family, rooted in the Word and work of God the Father, Jesus the Son and the Holy Spirit, bringing light, life and love to all. For as you open this book and step through this door, you will begin to discover **your** place of beholding, believing, belonging and becoming.

Embrace and enjoy the journey,

Dale Evrist
Founding/Senior Pastor
New Song Christian Fellowship
Nashville, Tennessee

Introduction

We live in a culture where instant gratification and pseudo friendships are a tangible reality. We have media, entertainment, drive-thru food, social media, instant loans, payday advances, store credit cards, text messaging, emailing, Facebook, and Netflix. And yet…we are further from feeling "satisfied" than ever before. We are saturated with what is easy and instant, and yet our souls are starving and malnourished.

Now, before you think this is a rant against technology, let us just chime in and say that is the furthest thing from the agenda here. We are sitting typing this on laptops with cell phones right next to us streaming music. No, this is much bigger than that.

Does your soul feel satisfied?

Does your spirit feel saturated?

Do you truly feel relationally connected? Like you're thriving, feeling known and like you know others at a deep heart level?

No matter how many movies you see, no matter how many TV shows you watch, no matter how many burgers you eat and new outfits you buy, no matter how many status updates, text messages, selfies, or newest hit songs you consume your time with, none of them will satisfy your spirit and soul the way they were meant to be satisfied.

You were created for relationship.

The need for relationship with God and relationship with others has been knit into your very DNA. You can't escape it, avoid it, or pacify it with other things. It screams to be satisfied. It cries out to be nurtured. And no form of attempted substitution will ever remove that need. That's good news! That's not bad news.

If you were created this way, and we all are, then that longing for more when this area is lacking is completely normal.

How about some more good news?

When God creates us with a need, He also provides a plan to satisfy that need. We need relationship, and He has a plan to fulfill that.

His greatest plan…drumroll please… is… family! That's right—family.

We suspect that even hearing the word "family" provoked some emotion in you on some level. For some people, you say the word family, and they smile with sweet nostalgia. If that is you, we are thrilled for you! If your next thought was, "my family is great; I don't need to read any further," don't leave just yet.

Maybe you are on the opposite stream, and the word "family" makes you cringe. Maybe it invites an instant sense of sadness, defeat, or a general sense of being uninvited. Please, don't leave just yet.

Most people fall somewhere in between with a sense of "I love my family; granted, they are a bag of mixed nuts, some of them crazier than others, but I love them nonetheless. I didn't have a perfect upbringing, but I came out relatively unscathed, and we love each other." You too, please don't leave just yet.

God's plans for family are multifaceted. We are born into a biological family, and we are also intended to function as part of a spiritual family—the family of God. No matter what your biological family looked like, you have a place in the context of spiritual family. All of us—every single one of us—has a place in the family of God. The adventure and joy comes in discovering where that place is.

Consider this your invitation to that journey.

One

Perspective

Rachel's Story

"I can't take it anymore. There has to be an escape."

Panic.

"It's too much. I can't do it."

Fight or flight.

"This is wrong! It has to be wrong! Does anyone care? Does anyone even see?"

This is what raced in my mind as I was running away. This is what churned in my soul as I walked alone that night through the seemingly indifferent streets of our small Northern California town. I was fourteen. Though outwardly I was trying to portray courageous defiance against the suffocating desecration I was living in, inwardly I was confused, scared, and utterly lost. I spent that night trying to find refuge somewhere, anywhere—temporary escape from the relentless sense of torment. I settled for the shelter of the abandoned middle school playground and spent the night attempting to sleep in an oversized tractor tire that served as a make-shift climbing structure.

I felt so lost between what my heart believed about the intentions for family, safety, security, love, and belonging and the reality of my very sobering experiences with family life day in and day out. I longed for a sense of truth, a compass out of the confusion and disorientation I felt in my soul. As the years went on, it had become harder and harder to rationalize against the experiential knowledge of daily life. Reality seemed to continually deny the authenticity of what my heart believed.

Hope had been all but extinguished, darkness seemed to be gaining ground daily, and I could feel my soul slowly dying. In an act of total desperation, I ran away from home. I had no idea where I was going. I had no money. No sense of a next step to take. No resources. I only knew one thing: if I could not escape the darkness, I was going to die there if not in body, most certainly in soul.

For me, the concept of family was such a source of ambivalence and confusion. I idealized the concepts of love, loyalty, and belonging, yet my constant experience was fear, shame, and rejection.

My mom and dad met in high school and were great friends. After my mother wound up pregnant, the baby's father quickly disappeared, leaving her abandoned. My dad married her so that she wouldn't have to face her future alone.

The child, my older sister, was born shortly after. Two years later I came along, and the initial impression would have led you to believe we were on our way to becoming a picturesque portrait of a family. That portrait lasted until I was about eighteen months old when my father came home and announced that he was leaving my mother for another man. Understandably, she was devastated. Our family portrait suddenly shifted. It turned from picturesque to shameful.

That shame was a constant companion until my mother met her next husband. From my observations, they weren't really in love with one another, but, rather, they met in the midst of mutual desperation and made an agreement to take care of one another. My stepfather was completely deaf at birth. He was one of eight children, and was born in a time when families didn't quite know what to do with deaf kids. When he was five years old, he was sent to live in a boarding institution for deaf children away from his family. There, he experienced harsh abuse as he grew up and was severely sexually assaulted by some of the older kids. As an adult, he still suffered from the inner torments that are born out of such situations. Six months into this new marriage with my mother, my stepfather began to sexually, physically, and emotionally abuse my older sister and me. One generation multiplied itself into the next, and the cycle of abuse continued, complete with pain, shame, and torment. This nightmare went on for years.

Two new sisters came along, sisters whom I absolutely adored and still do. However, nothing changed, and shame continued to rule our lives. We were ashamed of our poverty and of the fact that when my father had abandoned us, my mother fell into a deep depression marked by an obvious torment that seemed to consume her days like a plague of locusts. At five years old, an even greater force of shame and fear took root and began to govern our lives establishing itself firmly in the shadows of the sexual perversion and horrid abuse that raged within the walls of our house.

Family was confusing. How could someone love their mother so much while she seemed so disconnected from the trauma that was happening day after day, night after night in her daughters' lives? Cloaked in her own pain, she was blinded to ours. We went to church every Saturday, attempting to present ourselves as something holy and righteous. We put up a front. At home, however, lust and perversion were the daily agenda. The joy that came from the relationships I had with my sisters stemmed from a love as pure as any little heart could produce. I was eight. I experienced the purity every eight-year-old girl should experience in her soul. Yet, because of the abuse, I felt like the filthiest of prostitutes. Talk about confusing.

The concept of family was not at all redeemed the years after I ran away. I was sent to live with my homosexual father, and the notion of family found no redemption whatsoever. In fact, it was only further perverted, and it seemed as though any hope for something different became totally extinguished. My father lived his life through one agenda: selfish pleasure. Lustful sexuality, indulgence, and fear-filled self-focus were his compass for navigating life. This was true to such an extreme that later in life he went to Thailand to have a sex-change operation in order to further pursue his obsession with other men.

For years he launched direct assaults at my broken heart like flaming arrows. He constantly scoffed at my physical appearance. Over and over, he affirmed how undesirable I was. To him I was "ugly and disgusting," to be exact. He determined my worth through one lens: my sexual allure. Although I was only fourteen, my father obsessed over how sexually attractive he thought I would be to others. It took me years to realize that my father must have measured his own value through the same lens. No wonder he had never been capable of deep relational connection! My heart breaks for him still.

By the time I turned fifteen years old, my hope for the ideals of normal family had all but vanished. My focus turned to isolation and survival. I didn't know the Lord at all. I didn't understand the Father-heart of God. I didn't trust anyone, and I had determined to function through life with as little vulnerability as humanly possible.

However, that plan of survival fell apart by the time I was seventeen years old. I was lost. I had fully exhausted my own wisdom. Survival became simply impossible. I no longer had the resilience to stand up under the constant verbal assault and relentless disapproval from my father, and ultimately the Enemy. I attempted suicide. I gave up on family. I gave up on hope. I gave up on myself. I gave up on life altogether.

It was here that the merciful hand of God came in. He reached into the very pit of hell to rescue me, and my suicide attempt was unsuccessful. The following seven years; though, became a continuous struggle for survival, including one final suicide attempt that I miraculously survived. Then, when I was 24, I finally met and was radically rescued by my savior, Jesus Christ. That was when absolutely everything changed. That is when I began the journey toward God's heart.

I was quickly taken in and thoroughly loved by a precious family in my newfound church. They were, and continue to be, a beautiful source of God's redemption. I fell in love with God and His Church, and ministry soon became my whole life. I was desperate to embrace the idea that, in Christ, I was a new creation and sought to simply forget the first two decades of my life.

Sadly, because of this naivety in the spirit, paired with my fully-embraced inheritance of shame, I was not very discerning where ministry and church were concerned. I served on staff at my church in California for over six years. There I learned some incredible things about God. I also learned some disheartening realities about what happens in a church where there isn't a full understanding of God's heart for women, for healing and redemption, for the spirit of adoption, or for the concept of spiritual family.

Pouring yourself out in ministry without first receiving God's healing and love, no matter how pure your intentions, is like trying to water plants with an empty bucket. Even in Christ, I found myself confused and desperate inside. It was in this spiritually—and emotionally—exhausted condition that I first encountered the church community I now call family in Nashville, TN. I had come to visit a friend for the weekend and ended up feeling incredibly drawn to all the Lord was doing in this community. It was alive! The presence of the Spirit of God there was undeniable. Somewhere in the depths of my being; I knew this was a make-it-or-break-it time in my life. I asked the Lord for courage to lay hold of a different destiny. In one of the most radical acts of obedience to the Lord I have ever walked out, I moved by myself from California to Nashville only six weeks later.

I remember the day I walked into my first Sunday service. My heart raced with anxiety. I was overwhelmed with the idea of being at church, even though I loved the Lord. I had lost confidence about the Church's safety and integrity and wasn't sure I wanted to rekindle any hope in its promises. Add to that, my introverted self, who was overwhelmed at the number of people in the room, and if there would have been a way to become completely invisible or blend into the wall, I would have done it in a heartbeat! While everyone I met was as welcoming, hospitable, and southern as sweet tea, everything in my initial thoughts kept wondering if they were even real.

Due to the pain of my past interactions with the Church and the bondages of shame that cloaked me, I think it took about six months of Sundays before I could sit through an entire service without an anxiety attack causing me to make a premature exit. Yet something compelled me to keep coming: God. He was beckoning me back to full faith in Him, back to hope in His beautiful church, regardless of my skepticism and doubt.

Then there was the first time I heard Pastor Toni teach. It was actually the first time I had ever heard a woman preacher teach during a Sunday service. Her topic: the Church as a Family. Needless to say, God had my attention. It was the first service I was able to sit through without anxiety ruling my mind. There it was, two of the areas my heart most longed for—connection with family and the Church—being offered on a silver platter.

After being here for nine months, observing, laying low, and trying to allow my faith in the Church to be rekindled, I felt like the Lord was telling me it was time to take a step forward. Pastor Toni came to share one night at our young adults group, and I finally mustered up the courage to ask her if we could grab coffee or something. Before I decided whether or not I could fully re-engage with a church community, I had some pressing questions. We got together the following week, and I didn't waste a moment in laying my questions before her, nor did I hesitate about their intensity. I needed to establish a sense of safety. Pastor Toni was honest and gentle. And I felt at a loss as I sat there while my fears became diffused by her graciousness.

Then, suddenly, she turned the conversation around on me.

She said, "Okay, now that I have answered your questions, may I ask you some questions?" She asked me about my background, my involvement in the Church I had come from, what I felt passionate about, what I felt called to, and where I most desired to serve in the body of Christ. I was slightly startled that she would care to ask those things. The next thing I knew, all of these deeply honest responses came pouring out of my heart, and what followed was a great conversation about pursuing God's plan for your life and daring to believe Him.

That's when it happened.

That's when she said it.

That's when I felt a shift in my soul and spirit, an unprecedented jolt that had my attention. It was like hearing a gunshot at the start of a race and suddenly knowing you're supposed to be running!

She leaned forward and looked me straight in the eyes, the presence of God piercing through her striking blue eyes with absolute focus and intensity. She said, "Jesus went to the disciples where they were at and called them each saying, 'Come and follow Me.' Rachel, I feel this so strongly in my spirit right now. I am saying to you, 'Come and follow me.'"

I didn't know what to say. How do you respond to that? I had come in just wanting to make sure this place and these people were safe to do life with. I was asking how to dip my toes in the water of the shallow end. But this was something entirely different. She was asking me to jump off the high dive into the deep end. I felt undeniably gripped by the Holy Spirit. I felt excitement. I felt fear. I wanted to hug her and thank her for seeing me, I mean really seeing me. At the same time, I wanted to run out the door and never come back to this place. She was brushing up against the most vulnerable places in my heart.

Before I could think of something more eloquent to say, this horrific, I mean this really terrible, mortifying, I-can't-believe-I-said-it-out-loud question came falling out of my mouth…

"Um, Pastor Toni…did you smoke crack for breakfast?"

It's true.

I really said it.

I asked one of the most godly, loving people I have ever met in my life, this respected pastor, this daughter of the Most High God, one of the most crass and disrespectful questions!

It is even more mortifying now than it was then, but that was the honest response that came tumbling out of my lips. Did she know what she was saying? Didn't she see the source of the shame I felt was so apparent to everyone else? Didn't she know that the spirit of rejection had ingrained into me the belief that surely I wasn't invited to that kind of providence?

Even as I brazenly questioned her breakfast choices from that morning (okay, I admit, even as I questioned her very sanity) she was gracious. She just smiled at me and said, "At least pray about it."

I did pray about it. For a solid month, I don't think I prayed about much else. I knew it was God. I knew she was right. I knew He had something for me on the other side of all this fear. So I decided to take the leap. I chose to believe. I chose to follow.

Now, before I go much further, I will let her tell you this part of our story from her perspective.

Toni's Story

"Smoked crack for breakfast?" I (Toni) thought. "Hmm...well that just slipped right out didn't it?" I didn't even react to it, but I remember thinking it must have been a reflection of her past, her present, and her pain. She wanted me to know the gravity of her fear. That part I saw full well.

I remember vividly that first conversation with Rachel. She had recently moved to Tennessee from California and had asked me if we could meet so she could ask me some questions. I realized very quickly that she carried an incredible amount of pain and a definite mistrust related to her past church experiences and her family experiences. She primarily wanted to talk with me to ask questions—very pointed questions—regarding church leadership. They were valid questions, questions that needed to be answered in order for her to feel safe and to move forward within our church body.

I needed to validate her pain because it was real. She needed to know that the things she had experienced were not okay. As I tried to answer with as much honesty as I could possibly offer, I knew and could sense that she was feeling extremely vulnerable. Even though the situation felt very tender, toward the end of our conversation I felt assured by the Holy Spirit to call her forward. In the midst of that prompting from the Lord, I reminded her that when Jesus encountered Peter, James and John, He said to them, "Come, follow Me and I will make you fishers of men." I felt so compelled, especially in the midst of this tender moment, that she needed to know that the Lord saw her and that her destiny was still to be found in Him. I bid her to come and follow me.

She needed to know her worth, to understand her value, and to grasp the truth that she was worth pursuing. I was calling her out from among her peers saying, "If you will trust me, I will help lead you and guide you to Jesus. My heart toward you is pure. My heart toward you is to help you find the depth of the love of your Savior. I am committed to helping you find your way to the possibilities of a very different future in Christ."

At that moment I wasn't thinking, "Together we will discover God's heart for spiritual family, and I will be your mom and you will be my daughter." Rather, I was offering her an invitation to follow me as I follow Christ. I was promising to help lead and guide her in the days to come. It was, in fact, a commitment to serve her and love her. And because she fully opened her heart to that invitation, the Lord began to do much more than we had ever imagined. He was building a family for both of us.

We went from being mere acquaintances connected by a common church family, to becoming mentor and mentee, to truly receiving one another as mother and daughter. Now we are also great friends and partners in ministry. The Lord unfolded our relationship gently as we both pursued Him and the things of the Kingdom side by side. Rachel and I share a deep passion for reaching the next generation. We both feel called to counseling, pastoring, and ministering to people and relationships, and we have a fervent commitment to making God's heart and plan for "family" known. If you met us today, you would probably never realize we come from such different backgrounds; herein lies the beauty. You can see how powerful God's plans can be when you realize how unlikely of a pair we are.

Unlike Rachel, when I think of my family, my heart immediately warms and fills with sweet images and aromas of days gone by. I grew up in central Arkansas. Some of my favorite childhood memories include my mom's famous biscuits and chocolate gravy, the pink shag carpet I picked out for my bedroom (to go with everything else pink!) when I was thirteen, and those long dirt-bike rides on dusty gravel roads. I remember the excitement of summer church camp, spending long hours with friends, and laughing a whole lot! I used to get in trouble for laughing so loud (that really hasn't changed; some things never do!). But I have wonderful memories of my childhood and of the deep love and stability found within our home.

Both my parents came from strong Christian homes. They met when they were fifteen, married at sixteen and had me at nineteen. My mom had moved to the small community where my dad lived because her widowed mother had married a widowed minister with ten children. That's right, ten children. Adding my mom and her older sister made twelve kids. Because that wasn't enough, her parents had two more children, and this came right about the time I was born, bringing the final score to fourteen children. Talk about "Be fruitful and multiply!"

When I was about five years old, my young father became the pastor of a rural church that valued family, friends and strong faith in God. Our little house was right next door to the church. My mother stayed home with us (or rather she took us everywhere with her) and spoiled us with her love and affection, maybe even too much. I had two younger brothers whom I loved and laughed with, and also picked on and annoyed!

As I look back to that time in my life, I would say that the strongest gift imparted to us by our parents at the center of our faith and family was the value, power, and priority of prayer. I recall most nights hearing my parents pray strong, faith-filled prayers in their bedroom before going to sleep. I remember the comfort this brought to me and my brothers. My parents still carry on this pattern to this day.

Of course, we didn't have it all together, nor did we claim to possess any level of perfection. There were times of tears, regret and sadness. Ultimately, though, Christ and the Church truly were the center of our day-to-day lives and our solid foundation. Because of the impartation of my parents, I chose, at a young age, to give my life to Christ and have continued to grow in my pursuit and love for Him.

I graduated from high school and headed off to a Christian college for four years. I thought I would marry a minister like my Dad. I loved the thought of being a pastor's wife, since this was the only way I had really seen women work in full-time ministry. I had no concept of becoming a minister myself and marrying a man who would be called to labor in the marketplace, but to my surprise, that is exactly what God had planned. By the time I was in my early forties, I had become an Associate Pastor at an amazing church, serving under a strong male Pastor who was instrumental in releasing me as a woman into the fullness of God's call to the Church and to vocational ministry.

It was within this context that Rachel and I connected. When we first met, we had no idea that God was going to give us the opportunity to become family, nor did we imagine the adventure of ministry and partnership before us. One thing I particularly love about our partnership is that we share a God-given passion to help generations connect with one another other within the Church as they learn to love and be loved in deeper, richer ways than they ever dreamt possible. His church is not simply an organization. It is much more than that. It is meant to be a family. It is meant to be an entity where no one has to be alone, a place where one generation can train up the next as "spiritual sons and daughters" no matter what age or stage, and where the opportunity for the development and expansion of new family relationships never expires.

This book is so much more than a personal story. It is far from a testimony of one unique experience. It is meant to be a "how to" guide. It is a handbook for genders and generations to find one another and to learn how to walk out God's plan for love and family. This is what God designed the Church for to be family in every sense of the word.

You and I were created for family. Belonging to God's family is the ultimate expression of that inheritance. As pastors and counselors, we hear heart-wrenching stories of pain, abuse, loss and abandonment. God knew that sin would greatly scar and distort our perspective of His paradigm of family. He deeply values and desires that all His children experience that paradigm. Know this: nothing is beyond His healing. There's nothing He cannot save. There's nothing He cannot restore. As part of His church and His family, you undeniably, irrefutably and absolutely belong.

Prayer

Heavenly Father,

We pray over every person whose eyes will sweep across these words. We know, God, that You can see into the hearts of each one. You see them. You know them knowing even the very details of their precious lives. Father, we ask that You would bring revelation to their hearts about Your heart for them. Bring clarity to their minds about Your intention for family and Your desire for them to have this place of belonging, acceptance and love. Where there has been wounding, we pray You would pour out the oil of Your healing. Where there has been lack, we pray that You would redeem and provide. Where there has been disappointment and loss, Lord, we pray for an infusion of Holy Spirit-filled HOPE. Take each one of them by the hand and gently lead them to revelation as we journey together into these next chapters. We are in agreement with You, Father, for each one of Your beloved children to come to a greater understanding of Your heart for them and of Your intended provision for this very foundational need for family.

In the precious name of Jesus, Amen.

Two

What is Family?

I walked into the living room and found my five-year-old niece combing her hair with a dinner fork. Yes, a dinner fork.

She had recently fallen in love with Disney's classic movie *The Little Mermaid* and Princess Ariel. Ariel is an animated mermaid princess who is fascinated with relics from the human world and who is constantly on a mission to collect them. One day in the remains of a shipwreck, she finds a collection of new treasures, one of which is a dinner fork. She, along with her fish-pal, Flounder, takes the newfound treasures to their friend Scuttle the seagull who tries to identify the objects.

Scuttle informs Ariel and Flounder that the dinner fork they have found is, in fact, a "dinglehopper," which is used by humans to "straighten their hair out."[i]

"With a little twist here and a pull there, you have an aesthetically pleasing configuration of hair…," he demonstrates.

Later on in the movie, we witness Ariel employing dinner forks for this very purpose—hair straightening. Her innocence is charming and endearing, one of the marks of this entire film. It certainly captivated my niece.

What if we, like Ariel, thought that forks were for hair combing? Or what if we thought that shoes were only meant to kill bugs? What if we used a snuggie as a sled or a hairdryer as a hammer? Have you ever seen any YouTube videos of dads using vacuum cleaners to put their daughters' hair in a ponytail? Do you ever cringe when you see someone use their teeth to open a can of soda pop?

The magnitude of possible misuse when the intended functionality of something is not fully grasped, can be truly impressive.

What if family falls into this category? What if we aren't living in the fullness of what God has available for us because we simply don't understand?

It honestly doesn't seem to be a lack of desire for family that trips us up as a society, but a lack of definition and understanding that leads us to clumsily fumble through. Perhaps there is also a lack of willingness to honor the concept of family according to the integrity with which God created it. These two issues, our fundamental misunderstanding and our lack of valuing the integrity of God's intended family, plague us. They leave us paralyzed relationally and often isolate us from the love and the rightful belonging we are meant to have.

Have you seen the trailer for the movie *The Boxtrolls*? I remember seeing the trailer for the first time and being shocked with grief. It opens with an animated little infant boy standing in a street and the voiceover says in a loud voice, "Sometimes there's a mother. Sometimes there's a father. Sometimes there's a father and a father. Sometimes both fathers are mothers. Sometimes there's a mother and a father, a grandmother, a grandfather, weird aunties who wear funny hats, a butler, and funny uncles who eat rare, smelly cheese. And sometimes, there's no one at all." Then it proceeds to lay the foundation for the movie by introducing the boxtrolls who live underground and who adopt a little boy into their family.

Our culture seems adamant to define, redefine, and pioneer ever-changing definitions of the "modern family." You can sense society's desperation to maintain something called a family as a value. Yet, it seems as if we are grasping around in the dark to hold on to something we don't fully understand. Sometimes in that futile desperation, we create a definition that falls within our limited experience, not realizing the fullness of what God actually has for us in this thing called family. Regardless of how each of us has experienced family, we all have one thing in common—a longing deep in our souls to have and belong to family. It's no wonder we do since that has always been God's intention for His children.

What, then, is family? Merriam-Webster defines family as "a group of people related by blood or marriage."[iii] It also has definitions that include things like "a person or people related to one another and so to be treated with a special loyalty or intimacy; all the descendants of a common ancestry," or interestingly, "a group of people related by criminal activity." (Ha! This is not advisable!) There is even a definition for the more mathematically inclined: "A group of curves or surfaces obtained by varying the value of a constant in the equation generating them."

Needless to say, while Webster can offer us some semblance of understanding in the midst of our culture's confusing plethora of options, the real clarity about the critical components that comprise the authentic family can be best understood according to the criteria set forth by the One who first conceived the concept: God provides the only answer.

The first recorded problem in the history of mankind is found in Genesis:

> *And the Lord God said,*
> *'It is not good that man should be alone'* (Genesis 2:18a).

God had created the Earth and everything in it, and He called it good, but saw that Adam had no companionship. God responds to this lack with,

> *I will make him a helper comparable to him*
> (Genesis 2:18b).

It is not God's intention for any of us to be alone. Out of all creation, we are the ones created in His image, and God has never been alone. The Father, the Son and the Holy Spirit are all members of the Godhead (three in one). They are family. He designed us in that image, in His image. He designed us in such a way that to be alone violates our very personhood. Family is both the core of who God is and the answer to the human need for relationship.

God's definition of family is an ancestry, lineage, or a tribe.[iii] Much of the Old Testament places great value to knowing the lineage, the ancestry, and the specific place where people belong. There is great value, according to the Scripture, in being connected to the people with whom one shares a blood relation and heritage. God places a heavy emphasis on being related by blood.

In the transition between the Old Testament and the New Testament, Jesus, the Messiah, fully God and fully man, enters the scene, and the value of that blood relation transfers into an entirely different realm. God's value for being related by blood elevates to a whole new level. Only now, through the Messiah, the power of connection in His blood requisite for family transcends the blood connection which is passed down through generations of human family. Suddenly there is a whole new opportunity to be related by blood, to be called authentic family due to blood relation; it is found in the very blood of Christ. The blood of His sacrifice enables each of us to become grafted into the vine of His family, His lineage.

> *But now in Christ Jesus you who used to be far away*
> *have been brought near by the blood of Christ*
> (Ephesians 2:13).

Whether you had a great family like Toni or a challenging family dynamic like Rachel, there is now available an entirely different system of reference to the meaning of family. There are different rules. There are different definitions. There are different benefits and blessings. There are fresh, new promises, new dynamics. There is a new structure. To top it all off, there is an entirely new inheritance, one beyond our wildest imagination.

God's family is meant to be a place of belonging, a place where you are loved without measure, where you are valued, esteemed, cherished, celebrated, disciplined, taught and allowed to mature. Family is meant to bring a level of intimacy into our lives. It is where the details of our heart and our personhood are known and protected. Family is meant to be a lifelong commitment to journey through life hand in hand with others. It is a place to grow, stumble, make mistakes, receive instruction, find our way, practice expression of our individuality, and have accountability and structure. Family is intended to be the place where your heart is fully known and is fully at peace. It is God's perfect design for us to belong.

Not only is family about belonging, but it is also about identity. Within the structure of God's intended family unit, we begin to understand our identity. We cannot fully understand ourselves or fully become who we are meant to be without this piece of the puzzle. Dads impart masculinity and manhood to their sons. Mothers impart femininity and womanhood to their daughters. A father's protection and love of his daughter brings security and a sense of worth. The way a mother loves her son teaches him how to be gentle and tender. Parents are supposed to draw out the strengths and talents they see in their children as well as to steward within their children a heart of faith and obedience unto Jesus. Our families become an anchor of security that allows us to explore our gifts and talents while remaining tethered to structure, accountability, and responsibility.

Family is about authentic love. God's heart behind the creation of the family is one of utmost care and love. He means family to be an instrument of His care and love for us as well as a method for us to care for others. We are meant to be deeply loved and nurtured and also thoroughly equipped for selflessness. These deep bonds with one another teach us how to love the world around us to a greater depth. Ultimately, this unit called family is meant to draw each heart towards God Himself. The structure of family is very much a model for understanding the Trinity: God the Father, God the Son, God the Holy Spirit. All three function in mutual love, unity, and submission to one another, and unity not just for the benefit of each other but for the benefit of all mankind.

We would be hard-pressed to find anyone who has walked out his or her experience with family in a manner completely unscathed by the sin and depravity of the world. It isn't wrong to have a sobering, realistic perception of the state of our society and the imperfect state of the family unit. However, understanding reality does not mean that we must surrender hope.

This is the whole point of what we are doing together through this book. Our passion, our most sincere desire, is to provide a bigger picture of what family is. It is a two-fold picture—one that offers hope to redeem the brokenness of the past, and hope to impart the blessing of the wholesome family experience into the lives of others throughout the body of Christ.

The Creator of family, the Creator of the universe reigns eternal. The Alpha and Omega will not withdraw His hand from His children. The very One whose heart created the beautiful reality of family in the first place, is living, moving, breathing, and willing to lead us forth to the redemption afforded to us by His sacrifice on the Cross. God's desire is to lead us from what was or even from what is, to what can be—ultimately, to the perfect portrait of the redeemed family.

Prayer

Father in Heaven,

Give us eyes to see what You see where family is concerned. We are not satisfied with a lesser version than that which You have designed, created and destined for us. We long for You to establish within us the value of family and to not allow our hearts to be drawn to any version of family that is an abomination of what You have ordained. Help us to see what You see, hear what You hear, and feel what You feel about the multifaceted dynamic of family. Impart to us the perspective of heaven, and help us to embrace Your idea of family with faith and grace to receive it fully for the gift it has always been intended to be.

In the name of Jesus, Amen.

Three

Why Do I Need Another Family?

I (Rachel) remember going to church when I was a little kid. Everyone there seemed so untouchable, so unreachable, so…perfect.

The pastor's family would come in and sit in the same spot every week. There were seven children: five daughters and two sons. Every single one of them was pressed and polished. The boys came to church in suits, and the girls always had on the most beautiful dresses with matching hair bows and shiny shoes. They were beautiful. Their whole family was beautiful. I would watch them in wonder and awe from across the room. How did people get to be that beautiful? Even their hair was perfectly kept. And they were so well behaved. I couldn't imagine a single one of them ever getting into trouble. "What was it like to be so perfect, to lead such perfect lives?" I wondered. I observed. I was captivated.

At least, that was my perspective when I was seven.

Growing up, my interactions with the Church were quite interesting. I loved the idea of it, even from the time I was very little. I remember getting so excited when we sang my favorite song from the purple hymnals: the Battle Hymn of the Republic, page one hundred twenty-seven. I would stand up so straight and try so desperately to sing. Although it was far from being a joyful noise, even to the Lord, I didn't mind; it was sheer joy to my heart. We were all together, and we were there to talk about God. He was the most captivating, mysterious, intriguing topic to me. Although I had a smile on my face and hope in my heart that they would call out hymnal pages one, sixteen, or the beloved one hundred twenty-seven, there was still a level of confusion that remained within me.

See, with all my very best childhood analyzing skills, I was always trying to figure out just exactly what it was that separated "them" and "us." There were the beautiful church people, the ones who seemed to have perfect, wonderful, easy lives, and then there was, well, us. We were almost always late. My sisters and I may or may not have had our hair still in place after we made the forty-minute drive to church, and we may or may not have all found matching socks that morning. I know that the filthy things that were happening at our house, the abuse and perversion, couldn't possibly be happening in the lovely bedrooms of the pretty girls with the pressed dresses.

I wondered why. What was it about us? What was wrong with us? Their lives seemed so unattainable. I watched the way my parents interacted with the church community and knew very well that we weren't allowed to show our "real" selves to any of them. I was constantly on guard to know which parts of our lives were acceptable and which parts weren't.

I wanted desperately to be one of them. I didn't even know what that meant, but I knew I wanted to be one of them. I wanted to smile, to have pretty dresses with matching bows, and I wanted to see a smile on my mother's face that promised that all was well in the world. I wanted to go out to lunch with people in big groups after church. I wanted to be invited to the slumber parties, and I really, really wanted to go to camp. I wanted us, all of us, to belong and have permission to be real and still be okay.

My young heart just couldn't figure out the "why" behind it all. Why didn't we belong in the first place? My inability to gain accurate revelation through my seven-year-old understanding and reasoning skills led me to shame-based conclusions about myself, my family, and what God thought about it all.

Imagine the healing, the redemption, the restoration, the deliverance, the freedom—oh the freedom—that would have been on the other side of honesty, vulnerability, and grace! God's heart could have been made known. This is one of the reasons why we desperately need more than our immediate, biological family. This is why God's heart is for His Church, His Body, to function as family. Can you imagine the outcome and how different things may have been if our family would have had the courage to be real and had been met by other believers who had the courage to be real? Authenticity would have flourished. Belonging would have been experienced. We could have functioned as an authentic family within the greater structure of the family of God.

Obviously mine is just one story, one more reason why we need the family of God to function as a family and not as a corporate establishment. As the body of Christ, we need to look past our immediate definition of family, the definition that only includes the people who comfortably fit into our own minivans, our biological families, and find room in our hearts and lives for the extended family God has for all of us. But this is not the only reason. The perfect family, the one with all the kids in suits and pressed dresses… it was not until many years later when I found out about the deep sadness in their own lives. They had pain, struggles, and a reality that was far from perfection. They were much like the rest of us. It was simply that no one ever talked about those aspects of life, especially not the pastor and his family.

The premise of this book is certainly not based on one rough story, or even on the contrast between seemingly opposite stories, but on the eternal principles of God's Word. His principles apply to every person and every situation. His principles don't just offer hope to the disheveled, confused, church-going, seven-year-old version of me. God's principles and promises offer hope and encouragement for every life situation.

For instance, meet my friend Joel. Joel grew up with two absolutely incredible, godly parents. His father, who loves the Lord and lives his life completely sold out for the King and the Kingdom, is the founding and senior pastor over a church with multiple congregations. His mother is equally radically dedicated to the will, the ways, and the heart of God and has been for Joel's entire life. They were great parents, and they still are great parents. They are even fantastic grandparents, but in God's plan, Joel still needed more. Joel needed the fullness God had for his life through spiritual family, because in the dynamics of Kingdom, no one family has it all. No one family contains within itself everything a person needs to grow and fully develop into all God has in store for them to become. Joel's parents knew that, and they sought out spiritual family and a multitude of counselors to help mold their son's life from a very early age. Their wisdom was an act of love for which he is grateful beyond measure. And now he, in turn, will sow these seeds into the lives of his own biological and spiritual children.

Joel's Story

I've got a great mom and dad for whom I am so thankful. In an age of fatherlessness and widespread disintegration of biblically-defined family, it's rare to hear those words. There are no two people I genuinely respect more. There are no two people I'd rather spend time with, except perhaps my wife and kids. Mom and Dad's perspective on life thrills me. Their counsel and wisdom are of core importance to me. I love spending time in their home and staying current with what they're doing and learning. My mom and dad are now my friends. They're my comrades in ministry and my partners in life. Working together, laughing together, crying together over the needs of our people, and praying together—in almost everything—we do life together. Their covering and friendship are among my deepest joys.

I'm a pastor's kid. Pastor's kids get a bad rap—and for good reason! I've made many stout contributions to the "legend of the proverbial PK." I behaved poorly. My antics were mostly motivated by underdeveloped self-control. A big mouth operating disengaged from a big character got me my fair share of discipline. Ideas of fun conceived creatively when boredom surfaced bought me many sore bottoms. In response to my foolish actions and unfettered speech, I was always corrected in a home of consistency, love, and peace. Sadly, most pastors' homes are subcultures of their church lives. By subculture, I mean that life at home is different than life on a Sunday morning; there's different language, different priorities, values, and processes at home than a family might employ at a Wednesday night prayer meeting. It becomes difficult for a kid in a pastor's home to constantly switch "churchiness" on and off. Soon, they shrug the mask their parents wear and let their home education loose on the congregation. It's actually quite sad, and it is a difficult way to live.

This was not my experience. My parents were authentic, always the same people. There was no pretense, no weird transition from home to church or church to home. I can honestly say that I truly enjoyed my childhood as a PK. What's not to love when the word of God regularly comes alive in your home? Yet, my parents saw that they needed a strong team to help challenge me where they could not. I needed a covering they simply couldn't fully provide. They would regularly ask this question: "Who's on Joel's team? Who's going to partner with us and be an integral part of Joel's development?"

Paul, a premier spiritual father, said it best. He told his beloved Philippian family,

"Brethren, join in following my example, and note those who so walk, as you use us for a pattern" (Phil. 3:17).

Notice the words "those" and "us" in that verse. He and his companions were to serve as examples for the Philippians to follow. With Paul's inclusive intent in mind, he emphasizes a call for the saints to follow their leaders. He goes on to say,

"The things which you learned and received and heard and saw in me, these do, and the God of peace will be with you" (Phil. 4:9).

Paul essentially says, "Do the things we do to experience the things we experience." Not long before these two verses, Paul had told the Philippians that Timothy would be arriving soon. He describes Timothy as having, "proven character…a son with *his father [who] served with me in the gospel."* Not only would the Philippians benefit from Paul's ministry but also from Timothy's and from all those included in the *"us"* in 3:17. There was a team of folks pouring into the Church there. So, in like manner, my parents sought who was supposed to be on their team - on *"Joel's team."*

By the time I arrived at Bible college, to say that I had gaps in my understanding of life would be quite an understatement. There were things about God, people, and about the details of life I simply didn't know. Despite all my parents had taught me, there was infinitely more knowledge I needed to gain than I possessed. That's where my spiritual family stepped in!

My father modeled personal study of the Word and parented me by its truth. But it was my early Bible college mentor who coached me into becoming an ever-deepening personal student of the Word. My parents nurtured in me a love for missions. But it was our Missions Pastor who imparted to me a life-long fire for the global church. I overheard my parents counsel hundreds of folks in our home growing up, but it was the head of our church's Student Intern Program who imparted to me the skills and heart-attitude to become a biblical counselor myself. My parents were *wise, no-nonsense financial stewards. But it was our Executive Pastor who nurtured the skills of money management, living by faith in God's provision, and giving generously as a mature believer. It was our Young Adults Pastor who taught me how to never consider myself too "mature" to readily and humbly apply the truth someone can teach you. Our Kids Ministry Pastor coached me into a deep love for ministering to children. My Bible college instructors helped me hone my skills as a Bible teacher. My mentor during my internship at church helped me not to lose my sense of humor as I struggled with pride, taking myself too seriously. A close brother in the Lord taught me the value of physical fitness. Our Worship Arts pastors imparted the heart of a worship leader and songwriter. Our Small Groups pastor modeled gentleness. My childhood Kids' Ministry Pastor modeled patience. Our Church Administrator modeled responsibility. I had another sweet mother in the faith who modeled living prophetically. One of the elders at our church modeled biblical parenting and living to serve Jesus until our dying breath. I learned much from two of our younger pastors as they modeled the role of true sons to spiritual fathers in our church. Our Senior Pastor's assistant taught me time-management. Our Lead Evangelist imparted to me how to have a broken*

> *heart for lost souls. These people, among others, comprised "Joel's team." No matter our background, no matter where we come from, spiritual family is our inheritance. It is what God has provided for our spiritual formation, and it is what we desperately need to fully realize all His plans for us.*

God's principle and value of spiritual family is established in something far greater than individual family circumstances, and whether really good or incredibly dysfunctional, every family needs a community through which to survive. This is a universal truth for all—yes all—of His children. We all need each other.

No one understood this better than the Apostle Paul. Behold the man who is responsible for writing such a significant part of the New Testament. His heart and love for God and for His church is breathtaking and has given life to so many over the thousands of years we have read his writings. One of the most endearing things about the Apostle Paul is his heart toward those he pastored. He was a spiritual father through and through. He loved Timothy, his young Jewish understudy, as a son.

> *Timothy, my genuine child in the faith. Grace, mercy, and peace from God the Father and Christ Jesus our Lord* (1 Timothy 1:2 NET)!

> *But I trust in the Lord Jesus to send Timothy to you shortly, that I also may be encouraged when I know your state...But you know his proven character, that as a son*

> *with his father he served with me in the gospel*
> (Philippians 2:19, 22).

The Apostle Paul loved those in the churches he helped to pastor and fully considered them as sons and daughters in the faith. The tenderness and boldness with which he communicated with them absolutely exudes a father's heart. As believers, we not only benefit from the blessing of Paul's father heart, but we also receive instruction through his example on how to walk as mature disciples. A mature disciple is one who knows how to be a spiritual son or a daughter as well as how to walk as a spiritual father or mother.

The letters to the Thessalonians contain key verses on this principle. We will delve in to those in greater depth in a later chapter, but for now, we can see how Paul's words demonstrate this principle beautifully. Addressing the Church in Thessalonica, he reminds them of his general posture. He says:

> *We were gentle among you, just as a nursing mother cherishes her own children. So, affectionately longing for you, we were well pleased to impart to you not only the gospel of God, but also our own lives, because you had become dear to us* (1 Thessalonians 2:8).

He goes on to say in verse eleven and twelve of the same chapter,

> *As you know how we exhorted, and comforted, and charged every one of you as a father does his own*

children, that you would walk worthy of God who calls you into His own Kingdom and glory
(I Thessalonians 2:11-12).

Paul describes his relationship to the Church in images of a mother, a father, and their children. Why do we all need another family? We need spiritual family because it is the vehicle—the agent, if you will—that is required in order to equip us to walk worthy of God who has called us into His Kingdom and His glory. In addition to our own biological family, whether they have been the epitome of godliness, or the pinnacle of disgrace, we all need spiritual parents. In addition to our own children, whether they are models of well-pressed perfection or not, we all need spiritual children.

Prayer

Lord Jesus,

Let us walk worthy of You! What an incredible thought that You call us into Your own Kingdom and glory! Impart to our hearts this truth that to be called into Your Kingdom is to be called into spiritual family. Help us to see and embrace the JOY to be found in this truth, the LOVE it promises, and the HOPE it imparts. Let our lives be marked by fruitfulness, and let it be fruit that remains. Let us walk in courage by the Spirit to be willing to explore this Kingdom dynamic regardless of our preferences, comforts, or past wounds. There is so much promise of healing, of life, and of abundance in Your will and Your ways. Thank You, God, that You don't want us to miss out on ANY of Your promises and gifts. We receive Your heart and provision for us.

Be glorified in us Lord. Amen.

Four

God, Family & Me

I (Toni) was about ten years old. It was the Saturday night before Christmas, and there was so much excitement and anticipation in the air as we waited in semi-darkness for the annual church Christmas play to begin. Every single person involved was known and loved in our small, rural church family. They had practiced for weeks, and that night felt, to the children and even to some of the adults, like Christmas Eve. It was the event of the year in our tiny community.

My parents worked hard every year to provide a small gift of fresh fruit, candy, and nuts for every person or family in the room. This was not exactly a small task to prepare for over one hundred fifty people. Nevertheless, no one would be left out. Names had been drawn weeks before, and everyone would receive a gift from someone! Some families even brought their kids' Christmas presents to place under the tree at church, and these would be opened with everyone there at the end of the evening when gifts were passed out. This, the

Church, was their family, and it didn't make sense to do it any other way. There would be wrapping paper flying everywhere, kid's running and playing with their new toys, and so much joy and laughter filled the air.

No one had to convince me that church was a family. I knew it, and so did everyone else. We lived life together, both the joys and the sorrows. Even as a little girl I attended many funeral services with my parents because we lived life together—together at every age, at every stage, at every season.

Understanding the Church as a family was never a difficult concept for me, but I realize that this is not the reality for most people. For many, church is a place you go to with lots of other people you don't know in order to hear inspiring music and encouraging sermons that will help you make it through one more week; you go weekly to refuel. For others, it may be the place you have grown up in, and you have a few friends there and maybe some family members, but you don't know your own place, nor your fit, nor your purpose. Many of us are oblivious to the value and worth God has placed on family, let alone of spiritual family within the Church.

Think about this for a second: God at His very core is a family! He is three persons in one. We call this the Trinity—God the Father, God the Son (Jesus), and God the Holy Spirit, each Person having a distinct role and function, which are equal but different. His family is a perfect entity, a perfect nucleus of love, unity, purpose and submission. And this is our model. It is the purest reflection of an authentic, healthy family.

This truth is extremely compelling and even intriguing in light of all that Scripture has to say about this subject. Did you know that God desires fellowship not only with His Son and with the Holy Spirit but also with His earthly sons and daughters? He wants to be married to a special people and desires a pure, spotless bride for His Son. He prepared a special bride for Himself, a human bride, that His Son might be born through her, fully man and fully God, to save and redeem mankind. Ultimately, those who receive His offer through faith will be joined to Him as family forever and ever. He has literally invited us to be members of His royal family and joint heirs of His eternal glory with His Son. Seriously, that sounds kinda crazy! What kind of love is that? Just hang with me a little longer, and we will see how His very words will enable us to gain a deeper understanding of the greatness of the love He has for us.

*And we have seen and testify that the **Father has sent his Son to be the Savior** of the world*
(1 John 4:14 ESV).

*Yet for us there is one God, the Father, **from** whom are all things and **for** whom we exist, and one Lord, Jesus Christ, **through** whom are all things and **through** whom we exist*
(1 Corinthians 8:6 ESV).

Notice that our very existence is not only through Him but also for Him! Paul even says that those who belong to Him both in heaven and on earth have His name!

> *For this reason I bow my knees to the Father of our Lord Jesus Christ, from whom the **whole family in heaven and earth is named*** (Ephesians 3:14-15).

Furthermore, one incredible truth found in Scripture is that God desires to expand His family by inviting Israel to be His bride. He loves a big family!!!

> *"And it shall be, in that day," says the Lord, **"That you will call Me 'My Husband,'*** *And no longer call Me 'My Master,'* ***I will betroth you to Me forever;*** *Yes, I will betroth you to Me in righteousness and justice, in loving-kindness and mercy; I will betroth you to Me in faithfulness, and you shall know the Lord"* (Hosea 2:16, 19, 20).

> ***For your Maker is your husband,*** *The Lord of Hosts is His name; and your Redeemer is the Holy One of Israel; He is called the God of the whole earth* (Isaiah 54:5).

> *"Return, O backsliding children," says the Lord;* ***"for I am married to you.*** *I will take you, one from a city and two from a family, and I will bring you to Zion. And I will give you shepherds according to My heart, who will feed you with knowledge and understanding"* (Jeremiah 3:14, 15).

God the Father actually describes Himself as a faithful husband to Israel. Although she is unfaithful, He continually calls her back to Himself with a deep love and wooing affection. He desires her love and trust. One day she will acknowledge Him for who He truly is and will fully accept His offer.

Equally amazing is this: that we, the Church, are called to be the bride of His Son, and as such we become His family as well:

> *Therefore, my brethren, you also have become dead to the law through the body of Christ,* **that you may be married to another—to Him who was raised from the dead***, that we should bear fruit to God* (Romans 7:4).

> *For this reason* **a man shall leave his father and mother and be joined to his wife***, and the two shall become one flesh."* **This is a great mystery, but I speak concerning Christ and the Church** (Ephesians 5:25, 31-32).

> *For I am jealous for you with godly jealousy, because I promised you in marriage to one* **husband,** *to present you as a pure virgin to Christ* (2 Corinthians 11:2 NET).

Furthermore, the New Jerusalem in heaven is referred to as a mother, a bride, and the wife of Jesus, the Lamb. The Church is portrayed as this bride who is being prepared for her bridegroom, Jesus. One day she will live with Him in the beautiful city He is preparing for her, and He will bring this city and those living there to earth during the millennial Kingdom to reign and rule as joint heirs with Him for a thousand years.

> *Then I, John, saw the holy city, The New Jerusalem, coming down out of heaven from God, **prepared as a bride adorned for her husband**. Then one of the seven angels who had the seven bowls filled with the seven last plagues came to me and talked with me, saying, **"Come, I will show you the bride, the Lamb's wife."** And he carried me away in the Spirit to a great and high mountain, and showed me the great city, the holy Jerusalem, descending out of heaven from God* (Revelation 21:2, 9, 10).

In addition, the Holy Spirit also has a distinctive role in the family of God. He is described as the Helper, the Teacher, and the Comforter.

> *But **the Helper**, the Holy Spirit, whom the Father will send in My name, **He will teach you all things**, and bring to your remembrance all things that I said to you* (John 14:26).

Isn't it amazing to realize that, from Genesis to Revelation, God created, provided for, and purposed family for us, for Himself, and for His Son? Not only does He not want us to be alone, but He also doesn't want us to be lonely no matter what our family situation may have been in the natural. God created the first biological family, and He envisioned the Church to be not only His future bride but a spiritual family for His sons and daughters.

Nowhere is the depth of His love and tender care for family demonstrated more vividly than through Jesus' interaction with Mary His mother and with His beloved young disciple John at the foot of the cross. Think about this: Jesus is in the final moments of His life. He is in excruciating pain and is carrying the sin of the world in His body and His Spirit. He is about to die for the sins of all, yet in the midst of this divine moment in history, He is focused on caring for two deeply-grieving loved ones at His feet. He asks His mother to receive John as her own son and instructs John to receive Mary as his own mother:

> *Now there stood by the cross of Jesus His mother, and His mother's sister, Mary the wife of Clopas, and Mary Magdalene. When Jesus therefore saw His mother, and the disciple whom He loved standing by, He said to His mother, "Woman, behold your son!" Then He said to the disciple, "Behold your mother!" And from that hour that disciple took her to his own home* (John 19:25-27).

Jesus knew they would need each other in the days to come, but He was also leaving a profound example of the formation of a new kind of family that would be found in the Church. Where were his own brothers and sisters? Why didn't he ask them to care for their mother? We don't know for sure, but it seems that at that point they did not yet believe He was the

Messiah. Jesus was making sure those closest to his heart would care for each other, and we know from that day forward they did. In this, Jesus declared that spiritual family trumps even physical family if that physical family is not following the Lord. Jesus said his family were those who did the will of His Father (Mark 3:31-35).

> *With these supporters standing near him, Jesus focuses on his mother and the Beloved Disciple. Jesus says to his mother, "Woman, behold your son," and to the Beloved Disciple, "Behold your mother." Similar language was used in connection with betrothal and thus seems to signal some change of relationship. Jesus' mother is now brought under the care of the Beloved Disciple. In this Gospel there is a symbolic role for both the mother of Jesus and the Beloved Disciple, for they are both examples of true discipleship. So in changing the relationship they have to one another, Jesus is completing the formation of the community gathered around him-gathered around him precisely as he is on the cross. The new community is now seen to be a new family.[iv]*

How could we have lost this truth? How could we have misunderstood the provision of family within the local church when Jesus gave us such an example? It seems that in our present-day culture we have viewed the Church more and more as an institution, an organization or just an iconic, admirable building. We have reduced it to a simple gathering place where perhaps we may see a few friends, might receive some spiritual enrichment, or may even find a source of entertainment. Rather than the church functioning as a family unit in which every member participates and shares deeply held, common principles, it has become a mere shadow of what it was intended to be. In a healthy church, members are united in a bond of love that is deeply satisfying.

What if the Church became a body of "joint participants" of spiritual sons and daughters, brothers and sisters, and mothers and fathers? How much more rich and full would each of our lives become? What if the different generations in the Church found one another like Mary and John? What if we were willing to risk being hurt or disappointed in order to find our place in the family of God? Unquestionably, at the moment of salvation, we are born into the family of God. It is a reality that we can either embrace now, pursuing its fullness in this life, or simply treat as a spiritual reality that will only be realized in heaven. How much we will have missed in life if we settle for the latter.

The truth is, we will never experience the true fullness of the family experience outside the body of Christ. Those in the world who do not know Jesus as Lord and Savior have no hope of family beyond what they know in this very short life. Jesus gives us the Church as a spiritual family so that, no matter where we come from, no matter what our lives looked like before, we have a place where we belong. Having received Christ, we belong not only to Him but also to His eternal family. Belonging means engaging. We must engage what is being offered to us. Just because you attend church gatherings doesn't mean you have joined with the family. Just as watching a sporting event does not make you an athlete, attending a church does not make you a family member. You may be simply an observer, someone who is fed or entertained by what you see. By definition, an observer is someone on the outside looking in. Are you ready for more? Does your heart long to truly belong? You may be saying, "I really want to, but I don't know how." Let us help you find the way.

Our desire is to lead you, first and foremost, to receive revelation from the Father regarding His love and His provision of a spiritual family. We want to help you gain a much deeper understanding of these truths and guide you along with specific steps to take in order to walk this out. We want you well equipped to live life to the fullest in the context of church family. Jesus Himself wants you to experience the love He has for you, and He wants to prepare you to bring that love to others. Do not fear! Let your doubt be replaced with hope and expectancy. This is a journey of love well worth taking!

Prayer

Dear Heavenly Father,

We ask You to open our eyes and our hearts to the truth about who You are, not only as our Heavenly Father, but as our Father who created us to be in Your family, the Church. Help us to not settle for less than Your provision, but to find our divinely-assigned church family and make it our home. Help us to find our sisters and brothers, fathers and mothers, and even our sons and daughters in the Church. We acknowledge that we have a fit in the family of God that we must find by the power of Your Holy Spirit. Forgive us for not taking our place and for believing the lies of the Enemy that tell us we don't belong. Forgive us for making the Church a place we attend rather than a family we adore. We choose to embrace Your truth about family not any warped version we may have experienced. We also ask that You would help us to be patient with others who may also be learning this truth alongside us, and that we would do our part in being a family member for others rather than waiting to be personally pursued. We receive Your gift of family and thank You for providing a place for us to belong.

In Jesus' name, Amen!

Five

Calling All Spiritual Parents!

Before I (Toni) explain the concept of spiritual parenting, let's begin with the idea of what a *parent* is. When we say the word, *parent* it usually conjures up the simple idea of the people who birthed us as well as those who raised us. Simple enough, right? We actually have a very narrow view of the meaning of *parent*. Of course, there are many emotions behind the word *parent* and those emotions are filled with all sorts of memories, moments and messages we have received along the way. We tend to think we have one opportunity to be parented and to parent. We desperately hope to succeed, because if we fail, our life, along with the lives of our children, will be forever scarred. On the other hand, we can erroneously think, "Now my kids are grown. I did my best to lead them to Christ. My work here is done." Spiritual parenting is about way more than having 2.5 kids, being great "spiritual parents" to your own children (lots of good books written on that) and living out the "American Dream" until you get raptured and go to heaven (that, of course, is an entirely different book as well).

According to the Bible, parenting is about being fruitful and multiplying. This does not only mean that we fill the earth with people. It also means that we train up a generation that will love God with all their hearts, with all their souls and with all their strength! Unfortunately, most people are not parented that way. For those who are, it's clear to see the beautiful fruit that comes forth from that fruitful tree. But God is going to send the Church many children of all ages and stages who have not received biblical parenting. And He will send children who have received biblical parenting, but who still need the unique gifts and treasures found in "spiritual parents" to come into the fullness of who God has called them to be.

If we answer this call, we will have the opportunity to be richly and deeply involved in the lives of many and to greatly impact the next generation far beyond just our own biological children. I want to be clear here. We're not talking about foster parenting. Nor are we talking about the legal adoption of children. There are many books written on this beautiful call, and a relatively small number of people are actually called to and graced for such a ministry. What we are hoping to impart is the truth about what each of us in the Body of Christ is called to do. Within a church family, each member is to become an active participant in raising up the next generation of wholehearted, devoted followers of Christ. In so doing, we partner together with each biological family, and we become whole!

So what exactly do we mean by the phrase "spiritual parent?" In the same way that we are born into our biological family and inherit all the dynamics that come along with our physical lineage, once we are born again, Christ will lead us to spiritual family. Practically, we find our spiritual family within a specific church home, and we find our spiritual parents within that church family. There our hearts can be fully developed and come into alignment with our new spiritual reality in Christ. Just like a biological child should grow in development and identity through the guidance of their physical parents, a spiritual child should grow and develop under the loving reflection of Christ through their spiritual parents.

For the spiritual parent, there is a raising and releasing that takes place. There is a full measure of love and acceptance which is partnered with responsibility, coaching, and instruction. This process transcends the limitations of time as it ebbs and flows and grows through the stages of life in the Spirit. This relational dynamic may exist for a short season, a long season or for a lifetime. It may take place with one person, a married couple, or with multiple people within that church family, but it is intentional and purposeful in nature.

Basically, the practice of "spiritual parenting" is to provide biblical care and guidance for the heart and spirit of your identified spiritual children in a manner similar to the way you would care for and guide your biological children. The spiritual parent is positioned by the Holy Spirit to provide his/her spiritual children what they may have never fully received apart from Christ.

It's actually ironic that I, of all people, would be writing a chapter on parenting of any sort. My husband and I have been married for over thirty years and have had neither biological nor legally adopted children. It never occurred to either of us that we wouldn't have children when we got married. It wasn't that we couldn't have kids; we just never took the step to try, though we had numerous discussions acknowledging the need to "get moving on this." We loved children and have always adored our nieces and nephews, so it wasn't as if we didn't like kids. There simply was never the sense from either of us that "now is the time." I clearly remember about ten years into our marriage, when we were in our mid-thirties, saying to my husband, "I don't really have an urge to have babies, but I have this deep desire to have adult children, and I don't know how else to get them." We both kinda laughed and just moved on with life as we always did. Somehow we thought that one day we would get there.

Looking back, we now see that even then God had a special call on our lives. He would one day position us to deeply love and spiritually parent an ever-growing number of young adults. There would be many who would need our time, wisdom, love and attention in order to move forward in life. This is not to say that if we had birthed our own children, we could not have provided this. In fact, I have seen many parents of young and adult children provide this level of spiritual nourishment to others.

During those early years of our marriage, I was working as a family counselor at a wilderness treatment program for juvenile, delinquent boys. Never saw that job coming! I was not an outdoor-wilderness type, nor did I have any desire whatsoever to work with youth at that point in my life. One of the requirements for interviewing for this position was to spend twenty-four hours on the rustic campsite with the boys. I remember thinking I must be crazy for doing it, and I was certain that it would be very challenging in every way imaginable. I expected the teenage boys to be foul-mouthed, unmanageable, and rude to everyone they encountered. I had not expected they would run to me for affirmation, seeking a mother's love. That was precisely what they so desperately needed and deeply desired. I also never expected that my heart would fall in love with those boys that very night as they sat around the campfire sharing their pain and the shameful things they had done. Seriously, God has such a sense of humor! He knew all along that He had called me to love on and mentor other people's children. This God would do through me even if it meant putting me in such an unlikely place to begin my training.

As I am writing this, I am reminded of a fourteen-year-old boy who was placed in the program for severe behavioral problems. He came from a very difficult background, as you can probably imagine. Parents had divorced, addictions plagued on both sides, and the list goes on and on. He was such a great kid in spite of all that and really just needed someone to care about his life, someone to listen and to help him navigate his way. I really reached out to him as one of his counselors and could tell that his young heart became attached to mine. I remember getting a phone call informing me that his mother had been in a horrible car wreck and might not live. I had to tell him and take him to see her, which was incredibly difficult. I did my best to comfort him and care for him during that little sliver of time. We often talked about Jesus, although this wasn't a Christian program, and I hoped that one day he would put his trust in God.

A few years ago, this young man found me on Facebook. "*Momma passed. Sorry it took me so long to tell you. You held my hand that day we thought she wouldn't see another day. It's been nearly twenty-two years now. Thank you for being there for me. I am holding up well. Faith is all I have that carries me through really...*" Amazing! I was able to be his spiritual mom during those painful days of his young life, having no idea the lasting impact that would have.

In response, I said, "*I am so sorry to hear about your mom. I can't imagine anything more heart-wrenching. I remember her as a beautiful woman who deeply loved her son. You were blessed to have each other. I am sure she was proud of the man you have become, and I know you loved her so much as well. I know that God will bring you the comfort you need as well as the guidance for days ahead as you trust in Him. Thank you for letting me know, and reminding me of something that really mattered so many years ago. Much love.*"

Now, twenty-two years later, I could still affirm this man. Although in his thirties, I could still remind him of his mother's love even though he had watched her suffer through life-long addictions that caused him much pain.

This is the call of a spiritual parent. It's not the call to draw someone else's child to yourself for selfish motives but rather to draw that child to Jesus. It is a call to help each of God's children to know how to love their biological family more deeply and even to forgive, when forgiveness is needed. God will bring these precious ones to us, as the Church, in order to help them find the freedom they need to move forward in their walk if we are willing to invest in spiritual parenting or re-parenting them in the way He would desire. We have had the privilege of partnering directly with parents time and time again. Here is a testimony from one grateful mom:

Christy's Story

As a mom of two grown children, I have seen the Lord not only faithfully lead me, but also lead those I love. Many times, we will see Him use others in the body of Christ to pour out His love, mercy and healing. Often, there are people He will place in our lives for a season. But sometimes, He will turn those relationships into family. Even in our darkest hour, we can trust that He is a restorer and a redeemer if we are willing to let others have a part in that redemptive process.

My daughter, Christy, has become a true example of this restoration and redemption, as she has walked with family – both biological and spiritual.

When Christy was younger, she began to show signs and symptoms of depression. As she went through high school, it became clear that the problem was getting worse. The guilt I felt was almost unbearable the day I found her with an empty bottle of prescription medication. "What could I have done to prevent this?" I would ask myself. As a mother, I felt I should have been able to protect her. Although she was physically unharmed, that was a wake-up call. We knew something had to change. At her request, we allowed her to spend her senior year of high school with my sister and brother-in-law. They became spiritual parents to her. Looking back, I know the Lord orchestrated that year and used the family surrounding us to provide a place of healing and stability.

After high school, Christy attended college and would often come home. It was during this time that she began seeing a professional counselor. Full of compassion and wisdom, this counselor became a catalyst in helping her traverse a very difficult season. This came about in part through the counseling sessions and through an invitation for Christy to attend the church where, eventually, she would rededicate her life to Christ. This counselor became true spiritual family to Christy.

Christy graduated college and moved back home to Illinois for the summer. As she was determining where to live and work, we saw the Lord's hand unmistakably leading her to Nashville, TN. There, she immediately got connected with a great church full of people who were passionate about the Lord and who loved helping others become passionate for Him. After two years, the Lord led her to become part of an educational internship program within the Church that would train her for vocational ministry. This came about through various factors: her involvement with a life-giving host home, her partaking of Christian education, and the mentoring and training she received. As a result, Christy grew tremendously as a young woman in Christ.

One of Christy's mentors at the Church, Pastor Toni, opened her home to host Christy while she was in the internship program. She and her husband became instrumental in Christy's walk as she navigated through her next step in life: courtship and marriage. Even though the relationship with Pastor Toni began as a mentoring relationship for Christy, the Lord developed it into a true spiritual mother and daughter relationship. I often said to Pastor Toni that the Lord knew my daughter would need two mothers! I was incredibly grateful to have that partnership with someone in the Church who truly loved our daughter and wanted to see her grow in Christ. Their relationship made our relationship, as mother and daughter, grow stronger.

To this day, Christy, her husband, and their family

have a significant relationship with Pastor Toni and her husband, Kevin. They truly are family!

Through all the difficulties and victories, I have seen the Lord's hand work in my daughter's life, often through her connection to spiritual family. Today she is a wonderful wife, mother and daughter. This has been made possible through the love and support of various key spiritual family members provided specifically by the Lord. For that, I am eternally grateful!

You might be wondering where we would find this concept in the Bible. One of the strongest examples of this type of spiritual relationship found in Scripture comes from the apostle Paul's relationship with those he discipled and fathered in the Church. Paul actually refers to Timothy, his young convert-turned-pastor, as his son. Paul does not say of Timothy that he is "like a son" or "spiritual son." Rather, he sees him, by the spirit, as a "genuine child" in the faith. Here are some specific passages of scripture that speak to this issue of spiritual parenting.

To Timothy, my genuine child in the faith. Grace, mercy, and peace from God the Father and Christ Jesus our Lord (1 Timothy 1:2 NET).

You therefore, my son, be strong in the grace that is in Christ Jesus. And the things that you have heard from me among many witnesses, commit these to

> *faithful men who will be able to teach others also*
> (II Timothy 2:1, 2).

"My son" suggests, of course, that Timothy had been born into God's family by faith in Christ. As Paul wrote in 1 Cor. 4:15, he had "begotten" Timothy through the Gospel. The only way to enter God's spiritual family is by being born of the Spirit (John 3:1–6) and the word (1 Peter 1:23). Paul also refers to Titus, who was a Gentile converted by Paul to Christianity. According to tradition, he was consecrated by Paul as Bishop of the Island of Crete as a "true son."

> *To Titus, a true son in our common faith: Grace, mercy, and peace from God the Father and the Lord Jesus Christ our Savior* (Titus 1:4).

Paul truly saw himself as a father to those in the faith with whom he was personally connected. We can see his father's heart as he writes to the Church in Thessalonica. From this passage we will learn from Paul what He saw was most critical to being a spiritual father, along with the response of his spiritual children.

> *But we were gentle among you, like a nurse caring for her own children. So having great love toward you, we were willing to impart to you not only the gospel of God but also our own lives, because you were dear to us. For you remember, brothers, our labor and toil. Laboring night and day so as not to be an expense to any of you, we preached to you the gospel of God. You and God are witnesses of how pure, upright, and*

> *blameless we ourselves behaved among you who believe. As you know, we exhorted, comforted, and commanded every one of you, as a father does his own children, that you would walk in a manner worthy of God, who has called you to His Kingdom and glory* (1Thessalonians 2:7-12).

I love this passage of scripture because it so fully encapsulates the role and purpose of God's heart for what we are calling "spiritual parenting." I will speak briefly to each of these specific roles of spiritual parenting, as I find each and every one of them to be extremely important and greatly impactful in the lives of those whom God has privileged us to parent. I want you to read the list of roles first, and then I will flesh out each point with a bit of definition.

The Role and Purpose of Spiritual Parents:

- The Care of a Nurse
- Great Love
- Imparting of the Gospel
- Giving Our Lives
- Laboring
- Modeling Righteousness
- Gentle Exhortation
- Loving Comfort
- Godly Commands
- Kingdom Perspective

Care of a Nurse - We think of a nurse as someone who provides care and healing to someone who is sick or injured.

Most of the spiritual children God brings us fall into this category. First and foremost, they need someone who is willing to care for them and see them healed.

Great Love - The need to know and feel the deep love of another person who has no agenda other than a Kingdom agenda is profound. What we mean by "Kingdom agenda" is simply God's very own agenda for humanity. We have the opportunity to pour out the love of Christ on those, young and old, who may have never experienced that kind of selfless love ever before.

Imparting the Gospel - At the heart of spiritual parenting is the God-given desire to teach and impart the gospel to our spiritual children. To that end, everything we say and do is to be rooted and grounded in the Word of God. His Word and His truth must constantly be on our lips.

Giving Our Lives - Make no mistake, spiritual parenting is costly. It requires sacrifice. Our lives, our schedules, our preferences, and our time need to be invested for the sake of serving our spiritual children. Often, our sacrifice may be taken for granted, but without it, our spiritual children cannot grow.

Laboring - There is no better word that comes to my mind when I think about this process than "laboring." We labor with those God has given us in order to see the life of Christ made fully manifest in them. The process takes time, and it can be painful, much like that of a woman in labor. However, once the delivery happens, it brings great joy!

Model Righteousness - I have a responsibility to live my life in full obedience to the Lord and to model what a life fully surrendered to Christ looks like. I cannot give to another what I do not possess.

Gentle Exhortation - According to Webster, the word *exhort* means "to urge, advise, or caution earnestly; to admonish urgently or to give urgent advice, recommendations, or warnings." *Exhort* is one of those words can go in several directions. On the one hand, someone may exhort you in a way that feels deeply encouraging. On the other, someone else may exhort you in a way that feels deeply convicting or difficult. The truth is, exhorting can be both encouraging and challenging! How many unnecessary mistakes could be avoided in life if we would humbly receive advice, recommendations, and even warnings from those over us in the Lord? As spiritual parents, our responsibility is to exhort those younger in the Lord to avoid potential pitfalls in every area of their lives.

Loving Comfort - Much of the role of the spiritual parent is to comfort the brokenhearted and to help to bring healing from all of life's pain and disappointment. Above all, it is simply to be there, to stand alongside those we shepherd, no matter what.

Godly Commands - Spiritual parenting, of course, is not all about comforting. It's also about correcting and bringing hard, honest truth regarding the narrow path Christ has called us to walk. It's having the courage to call out sin and being forthright with the truth of God's Word.

Kingdom Perspective - A huge part of our role is to impart a Kingdom perspective. We must help our spiritual children focus on that which is eternal. We need to take the far-sighted view knowing that we must teach them about reigning and ruling with Christ based on our love and obedience to Him in this life.

Over the past fifteen years, God has entrusted me and my husband with the spiritual parenting of dozens of sons and daughters in the faith. We have had over ten different single, young-adult women live in our home for anywhere from a few months to a couple of years as they prepared for ministry life and marriage. Some remain extremely close to us to this day, while others have moved on and have not needed our ongoing support on such a deep level. In both cases, we rejoice! Most of them have married, and some have children. We have had the privilege of shopping for wedding dresses, providing pre-marital counseling, and shopping for cars. We've cried over broken dreams and have even been in the room when babies were born. I would never have imagined the fullness of all this blessing. I am in awe of the Lord!

Just this past year we had the honor of being the "parents of the bride" for our dear daughter in Christ, Rachel. And all because we embraced this call to pour out our lives for those God called precious in His sight. This is something we never dreamed of! What an incredible privilege He has bestowed upon us! I could never have imagined seven years earlier, when this very broken young lady entered our church, that she would become not only a daughter in the deepest sense of the word but also a dear friend and ministry partner. It is she who now coauthors this book with me on spiritual families!

As it is in everything with God, the rewards always go far

beyond the sacrifice. There is much to be received in return, time and time again. And the blessing is not just for us. It's available to all who will avail themselves of the heart of the Father to parent many more than we could have ever imagined, because His love is worth pouring out and reproducing in others. Ask the Father to let you feel His heart for family. Ask Him to help you to be willing to pay the price to parent another generation. Why do we do this? We do this because He has given His all for us, and He is worthy of all our love and adoration. He came to set the captives free. He wants to use us in even greater measure than we have ever known, as we embrace His call to be spiritual parents. The capacity is in you! Embrace Him! Embrace them! They will come and follow you as you faithfully follow Christ.

I invite you to pray the following prayer with me.

Prayer

Dear Heavenly Father,

Thank You for the privilege of being loved by You! I know that Your love is to be poured out through me to others, and I am asking You to do that work in me. I want to open my heart and my life to spiritual sons and daughters who desperately need the love, wisdom and care of spiritual parents. Please remove all fear and doubt from my heart. Take away any intimidation that may be in me towards those of a younger generation or thoughts that my life is already too full with other responsibilities. I want to walk in Your peace knowing that Your grace is sufficient, and that I will actually be blessed beyond words to have my "quiver full" of spiritual sons and daughters who love me and trust me to help lead them to You in every area of their lives! You deserve their loyalty and love, and I want to be a part of raising up the next generation of Christ-followers alongside their biological parents who love You! Help us see we need each other, and that it is by Your design that we do. Open my eyes, even now, to see those You may have put right in front of me who need my love and counsel. What joy awaits me as I fully embrace this call from Your heart to mine! Yes Father, I say yes! By the power of the Holy Spirit, Amen.

Six

Calling All Spiritual Kids!

One of my (Rachel's) favorite pictures from my wedding day is one that someone snapped of me and mom. All the hustle of the morning was nearly over; the bridesmaids were all in the upstairs hallway decked out in their elegant, slightly-sassy dresses. The bouquets had been delivered. The rest of the family and the bridal party were on their way, as pictures were about to begin. Dad was on his way up to the room for a first look at the bride. My hair and makeup was just about done. I had just finished getting into my dress, checking to make sure everything was in place, when I caught a glimpse of my breathtaking mom. She had just finished getting all gussied up herself, and she was standing there in the beautiful, elegant, eggplant-colored gown we had picked out for her. She was stunning. I could feel the tears welling up in my eyes threatening to destroy all the effort it took to get those pesky false eyelashes just right. She took my breath away. She looked at me and said, "Oh wait, your lipstick!" She grabbed my lipstick and came over to help me put it on since there was no longer a mirror nearby. That was the captured moment.

It was such a picture of her heart. This is who she is, my beautiful spiritual mother, totally unaware of her own beauty, and of how her love beautifies those around her. She has spent her life serving the Church and seeking to prepare the Bride of Christ for her soon-coming King and Groom. She lives and loves sacrificially. She pours herself out for the sake of the Lord, with no hesitation or reservation, on a daily basis. And in that moment I was overcome by the overwhelming assurance and knowledge that she was mine. Earlier that morning I had a similar moment with my spiritual dad as I woke up to a card he had slipped under my bedroom door. It read: "To the bride from her father on her wedding day." The sweetness of their presence on that day ministered to my heart in indescribable ways. The Lord brought us together as family. They chose me. That knowledge reduces me to a puddle of humble gratitude on a regular basis, but it hit so much deeper on my wedding day. Since I was a little girl, I had never really dreamed of having such a beautiful wedding. It felt like a fairy tale. Never in a million years did I dream I would have parents who would fully embrace and receive me as their own. But they did. My reality was better than a fairy tale. It was better than a movie. It was real life. Through them, God was showering me with more love and redemption than I ever dreamed possible.

This is possible for you. Yes, for YOU. This was not just a fluke or a simple stroke of luck, like winning the lottery. This is what it looks like when we reach out to receive the love and redemption the Lord offers through church family. His heart is to have everyone experience this aspect of His character. His design for His church is that she would minister His heart of adoption. God in three persons, the Father, the Son, and the Holy Spirit, is a structure that exemplifies family. This is who He is. He sent His Son to teach us about the Father. We cannot fully understand ourselves, our purpose, or our destiny, outside of our identity within the family of God. O that we could grasp the depth of this portion of our Father's heart! We were created by Him and destined for family, just as we were designed to need water to stay alive. That longing cries out within us, and we feel disoriented without it. Just like we must reach out to drink a glass of water, we must proactively reach out to grab hold of a spiritual family. It is a God-ordained dynamic our soul needs stay alive.

These moments I now share with you, these deeply impactful moments and memories, weren't born overnight. They didn't happen accidentally. They weren't chance or happenstance. They are a reflection of an intimacy that was built over time. They are evidence of an earnest effort on both parts. There is a sweetness in them that came only through all the hundreds of moments that came before them—moments when incredible vulnerability encounters a courageous willingness to trust. They blossomed from moments of risk where your heart is exposed and your pain and rejection are on full display. It is here that those past hurts can be met with the tangible power of tenderness and the incomprehensible potency of love. Real relationship is risky business.

So how do we get there? How do you walk from where you

are at right now into these moments of love and fullness? How do you go from walking in the front doors of a church building and into the heart of church family? Let's talk about some of the practical steps.

Trust

The first step is to have an understanding of how to build trust. No matter how exemplary and wonderful your life may have been, no matter how devastating or disappointing, every human being has to encounter and reconcile the delicate fragility that relationship entails. Building trust within this delicate environment is the overarching theme of all the steps we will unfold throughout the rest of this chapter. Each aspect feeds into the establishment of real trust.

To begin with, before you can practice the art of building deep trust with spiritual family, you need to have a fundamental understanding of trust in the Lord. Building trust and establishing relationship are rooted in understanding and experiencing safety. That safety and security must first be established in your relationship with God. This sweet comfort and assurance of safety and security in Jesus is His provision to protect any accidental relational wounds from damaging your sense of value. Your sense of value and belonging has to be firmly identified in Christ in order for you to feel a tangible safety to relate with others. For some, this may be an easy concept and practice. But for the majority of people, this is the hardest part. Trusting God and feeling safe may be part of the underlying sense of unrest to many of your relationships. Fear not! We are not expecting you to already have mastery over this subject. However, we feel it is imperative to establish its importance as the foundation for building other relationships.

Relationships with spiritual parents are critical to the fullness and abundant life in which we are encouraging you to engage. They are also a significant part of understanding and walking in your God-given purpose and identity. In order to build the kind of trust that will create an atmosphere that encourages the risk involved in relational depth, it is imperative that we understand our source as spiritual beings. Jesus is our source. Spiritual family is simply part of the way God provides us the opportunity to blossom into all aspects of that which He has already approved and appointed.

Start with prayer. Bring this issue before the Lord as a point of conversation, and ask Him for revelation, understanding, and guidance through the process. Confirming your trust in Christ is where the courage to establish trust with others is born. There is no safer place in the universe than to be tucked under the shadow of the Almighty.

> *He who dwells in the secret place of the Most High, shall abide under the shadow of the Almighty. I will say of the Lord, 'He is my refuge and my fortress; My God, in Him I will trust'* (Psalm 91:1-20).

He is our shield and our buckler. When we give Him our trust first, it creates a haven from which we can offer our trust to others.

The following is a model of prayer that can help set you on the right course:

Heavenly Father,

Thank you that Your Word promises that You will be my refuge and my fortress if I will choose to put my trust in You. From this day forward, I choose to put my trust in You. Thank You that You are trustworthy. You value the fragility of my heart and soul. Thank You that You desire to be the source of safety from which I can relate to others. I receive You as this source, Lord. I pray that You would impart revelation to my heart on this topic of spiritual family. I pray for understanding and wisdom as I seek to navigate through this part of my life in Christ toward fullness and abundance. I pray that You would help my heart to be firmly rooted in the safety of Your love, first and foremost. Open my eyes to see specific people who may be carrying spiritual keys for me in this season of my life, keys that would unlock the doors of my heart, that I may receive the full provision of family that You have for me. I pray that, regardless of my past relational history, You would impart to my heart courage, gratitude, and willingness to embrace this truth of Your plans and provision for me. I receive Your love for me, God. I pray that You would pour it out over me in full measure.

In Jesus' name I pray, Amen.

You will find great comfort and encouragement on this

journey if you will employ such prayers through each stage. Please be encouraged that the Lord cares about every fear, concern, wound from your past, and hesitation about your future. Bring your burdens to Him in prayer. Lay them at His feet. Allow His comfort and peace to be your constant companion as you seek to embrace spiritual family. After all, this was His idea.

Identify

Now, with that foundational piece in place, let's talk about the big looming question: "How do I find my spiritual parents?" It is not as if there is a spiritual equivalent to the local mall where all you have to do is decide whether to shop at Macy's or JC Penny's. Nor will a heavenly stork place spiritual parents on your doorstep. The good news is we don't decide on our own where to go to expose the most vulnerable parts of our heart. (Good grief! Some of us even struggle to decide what to wear today!) There is no need to worry. Finding spiritual parents is not something forced on us that we have no voice in, like paying taxes. Quite the contrary.

Where else would you be led to your spiritual family, and they to you, other than by the very loving, provisional hand of God? Listen to the heart of Jesus on this, straight from the red letters in the Gospel of John:

> *Peace I leave with you, My peace I give to you; not as the world gives do I give to you. Let not your heart be troubled, neither let it be afraid* (John 14:27).

O dear ones, let His heart penetrate yours with this promise:

I will not leave you orphans (John 14:18).

If you are willing to receive spiritual parents and willing to embrace being a spiritual son or daughter, He will provide them for you. He longs to do this! He is more excited to give this incredible gift to you than a child is to receive presents on Christmas morning!

However, put first things first on this process of discovery. For starters, you have to get plugged in to a local church family. It's kind of like people who want to get married. They have no prospects but don't want to get off the couch to meet people—it's just not going to happen that way. In order to discover church family, you have to put yourself out there. You have to attend the Sunday services, get plugged into the small groups, go to the young adult ministry events, etc. You can't become family without first meeting people. If you are introverted, take a friend with you. Sometimes courage comes in numbers; that is okay! Bring a friend and show up to stuff! That is the basic first step.

Next, you need to know that you not only have permission but are encouraged to guard your heart carefully.

Keep your heart with all diligence, for out of it spring the issues of life (Proverbs 4:23).

To engage in this process does not mean you allow anyone and everyone access to the depths of your heart with no regard for their trustworthiness. Nor does it mean that you erect walls around your heart that make it impossible for people to get through to you. In order for the purest of loves and the best intentions to reach you, you must be willing to let down your guard. There is a balance. You guard your hearts knowing they are precious, while carefully considering those who the Lord may be calling you to relate to on a deeper level of trust and connectedness.

The Scriptures provide a very concrete safeguard for making the determination of who should have that level of access.

> *Even so, every good tree bears good fruit, but a bad tree bears bad fruit. A good tree cannot bear bad fruit, nor can a bad tree bear good fruit. Therefore by their fruits you will know them* (Matthew 7:17-18, 20).

We have to pay close attention to people's character, their actions, attitudes, and their heart towards God and others. What fruit is evident in the people around you? Does it draw you to Jesus or to the things of this world? When you witness people who are prone to anger, sarcasm, selfishness, and gossip, does it make you want to draw near to them? However, when you see people who are giving, kind, patient, and loving, it makes you excited to spend time with them. This is why we recommend that you evaluate the wisdom of relating to certain people according to the fruit of their life. Ultimately, you are looking for people who walk in the demonstrated fruit of the Spirit of God.

> *The fruit of the Spirit is love, joy, peace, longsuffering, kindness, goodness, faithfulness, gentleness, self-control* (Galatians 5:22).

People who are trustworthy bear such fruit.

Next, ask yourself this question: "Who here, within our church community, is walking in the fruit of the Spirit? Among these, who would I want to emulate?" The first conversation I ever had with Toni, my spiritual mom, didn't begin with some huge embrace of love. There was no deep eye contact, no request for her to become my mom. That would have been awkward, right? My notice of her (not in a creepy stalker kind-of-way) began long before we ever had a conversation.

She was on the platform preaching one Sunday morning when I really saw her for the first time. I remember thinking, "Who is this dynamic woman preaching?!" Something awakened within me, and I felt drawn toward the things I saw in her. Something about her being fully herself in the Lord called out to similar giftings and callings in me that had yet been fully realized. The reflection of who Christ was in her began to stir those things in me. I caught a glimpse of someone from whom I could learn how to more fully be myself.

God wants us to courageously and boldly engage in relationships where the fruit of His Spirit is evident. His leading will guide us. As we delve into the next chapter, we will discover the practical steps we can take to this end.

Expectations

Because this is uncharted territory for so many of us, it is important to establish appropriate expectations. This may honestly be one of the trickiest elements to navigate. Relationships are a tender thing. Our hearts cry out for the freedom and the liberty to give and to receive the full expression of love within our God-given potential. It is imperative that we seek the heart of the Lord for healthy expectations in every relationship. We must be careful not to swing on a pendulum ranging between being nonchalant to being co-dependent. We don't want our heart attitude to reflect ingratitude, nor do we want to be suffocating. Someone who comes from a healthy family with great biological parents may have certain expectations that come across as entitlement because they are used to being loved, valued, and attended to. On the other hand, those who have never had a great relationship with parents may have been so starved for love and affection that they can tend to hold on too tightly out of a fear of abandonment. We want to avoid both extremes.

This statement may sound like something that would be heralded by Captain Obvious, but I am going to go ahead and say it anyway: spiritual parents are people too. One of the most common revelations I have seen bring peace to the hearts of so many spiritual kids as they are learning to embrace being spiritual kids is the realization that the people who are pouring out their lives in love to parent them are actually human. Believe it or not, spiritual parents are human! They have feelings, they need encouragement, they need your prayers, and they need you to know they can be fallible. Don't hold your breath waiting anxiously for them to err.

Their error will not invalidate the process or render it "too good to be true." It will happen faster than you think. They will make mistakes, and you will be disappointed.

Your expectations, therefore, need to be grounded in Christ. The understanding that no one but Christ is perfect will grant you freedom. We all need compassion and understanding from others, even our leaders and parents. You would be hard-pressed to find anyone who would stand up and claim to be the perfect, most amazing spiritual parent. Many may be slightly apprehensive right alongside you. They, too, are aware of their shortcomings. Yet they are fully committed to walking in self-sacrifice and to pouring out their love and their very lives to be to you what the Lord is asking them to be. Everyone's heart can be at ease. We all have permission to be imperfect.

Another way to walk in healthy relational expectations is to guard yourself against fantasy. This will be especially true if you grew up experiencing the trauma of omission – meaning that you feel a sense of trauma in your soul for all the things you were designed to receive in order to grow and mature in a healthy manner, but which never came to pass. Sometimes we experience a level of trauma in our heart, mind, and soul from what we didn't receive. The Lord's heart is very tender towards this. He knows you haven't received what you should have and wants desperately to heal those parts of you. Please hear this: those needs are still incredibly, irrevocably valid, and God's heart is to fulfill and mend each and every place of loss. The key to receiving that healing is to understand that God is the Great Physician. He is the Healer. If we seek to heal ourselves or seek to control outside relationships in order to facilitate our own healing, it will backfire and lead to further damage to our souls. We can pray, lay those needs at the feet of Jesus, and walk in faith for Him to be the orchestrator of relationships and author of healing.

Toni and I both have counseled spiritual families who struggle in this area. We have encountered parents who pour themselves out with extravagant love. They offer everything they possibly can to establish safety in the lives who claim to desire parental relationship. Yet, despite their efforts, they are met with a wall of continual distrust and a sense of disappointment from the ones to whom they offer themselves. On the other side of that are the spiritual kids who have experienced such lack in these relational roles that they have constructed a fantasy in their minds of what it must have been like for everyone else.

False expectations grounded in fantasy can never be fully met by anyone. This is a scheme of the Enemy to keep so many people bound in the lie that they will never belong, never be fully included, and never be truly loved, when God's desire for His people is fully the opposite. The same kind of thing can happen in so many relational dynamics. A huge area this can be seen in is the realm of marriage relationships. So many people stay single for so long because no one can meet their expectations, expectations which are so often rooted in fantasy. We have seen too many movies, scrolled too many Facebook pages, watched too much TV, and daydreamed too often to find the value in the incredible gift of reality. If we can't see with eyes of reality and welcome relationship with a heart satisfied with that reality, we will miss the incredible gift of Jesus found in others.

There is extraordinary beauty in seeing the imperfections in my spiritual family. I see their quirks and flaws. I see their weaknesses and fallibility. I see *them*. It makes their offerings of love that much sweeter to me. I know they are walking in the faith that Jesus will use their offerings of love to minster to my heart. This refreshing perspective that allows them to be their real selves also allows me to respond back to them in the way I relate. They are human. So am I. The Holy Spirit works in the midst of all the flaws to make us feel loved, valued, and safe. It's a wonderful tapestry of beautified imperfection.

I'm going to share this with you, and I want you to hear it from the heart of a big sister pouring her heart out to you right now. It is not the responsibility of spiritual parents to make amends to you for everything you didn't receive. It is not their responsibility to repay you for what was lost. Those are things that God alone can heal. He often uses spiritual family to play a role in that, but no one person holds all the keys for us. Jesus is the only One who holds all the keys, but He often uses the Body to open up those places of healing for us. We need moms and dads, brothers and sisters, covenant comrades, our own spiritual kids, pastors, mentors, and leaders. Hear His heart: He longs to heal those places. As He does this healing work, ask Him to show you what is healthy to expect and not to expect. Like I said earlier, keep that priceless heart of yours tucked safely under the shadow of His wing.

A Map for Your Journey

If there was one gold nugget I could give you to encourage you on your journey into spiritual family, this would be it. I want this truth to echo in your ears as you take your next steps: honor paves a wide path. Give honor. Do this well, and there will be so much grace and mercy for mistakes you will certainly make along your relating path. If you come into the realm of relationships with a heart that is only searching for what is in it for you, you will be missing one of the most fulfilling aspects of relating in the Lord. No matter where we are in our growth and process in the Spirit, we have something to bring to the table. Set your heart on giving, serving, and participating in relationship.

It is what we call a "poverty mindset" to come into relationships primarily seeking what is in it for you. It is a mindset based on lack, viewing life primarily through a lens of what you don't have. Poverty mindsets lead to empty, impoverished relationships. Rich relationships are the inheritance and ways of royalty; and if you, beloved, are a child of the Most High God, then you are indeed royalty. A heart set on giving honor and respect to others is a heart grounded in the reality of being part of the royal family of God. Set giving honor as the goal before you. These are Kingdom relationships to be treated as royal treasure and conducted in a manner reflecting honor, dignity and respect. Romans 13:7 says to give honor where honor is due. All believers are part of the royal family of God, so have that mindset as you approach the Body of Christ.

The well-known scripture in Exodus also reminds us to:

> *Honor your father and your mother, that your days may be long upon the land which the Lord your God is giving you* (Exodus 20:12).

Certainly, this applies to your biological father and mother. It also applies to honoring those who have gone before you in the Lord, including fathers and mothers in the faith who have paved the way for us. As the Lord leads you to discover who your specific spiritual mothers and fathers are, make sure you enter into those relationships with a heart set on honoring them for who they are in the Lord.

To honor someone has many implications. Many books have been written on this topic, so we will not take time to fully expound on the topic of honor here. However, there are some key takeaways that may be helpful. Honor is about holding someone in high regard or reverence. It is showing courtesy and respect. It is walking in a manner that communicates devotion and worth. Honor is dispensed in degrees. It is never dishonest. It never requires you to function in a way that denies reality. You can communicate honor to your parents, both biological and spiritual, by the way you walk with Jesus. Honor is about treating someone as important and valuable. Make sure that as you engage in these relationships, you are simply communicating the value you hold for the people in your life and respecting the role they have in your life.

This is an incredible adventure, spiritual family. With Jesus at the helm, you will discover blessings at every corner, love that overwhelms and surprises you, joy that wells up within you, and peace that washes over you. When it all truly hits the mark the way He intends it to, you will end up with a heart so full of gratitude that it will compel you to pour yourself out in like manner for another. That is simply the beautiful way of the Kingdom of God.

Prayer

Father in Heaven,

We pray over every son and daughter of Yours who is reading this now and over those who are endeavoring to lay hold of this beautiful provision of family that You promise to provide. Holy Spirit, pour out Your grace over them on this journey. Encourage them to trust. Give them eyes of faith to see the specific family members with whom You are calling them to walk out life. Help them to have appropriate, healthy expectations of what relating should look like as they seek to relate in the realm of Your family dynamics. Teach them and anoint them to walk in Your ways of giving, respecting, and honoring. Above all, Lord Jesus, open their hearts up to receive and embrace this beautiful, amazing, incredible aspect of life in the Spirit, that their hearts may overflow with Your love poured out over them.

Amen.

Seven

Who Asks Whom to Dance?

Practical Steps for Relating

One of the words I (Toni) hear used quite often among the Millennial generation is the word "awkward." I have heard them say it so many times and use it to describe many different situations that lack social graces. It's usually followed by the description of a very strange or funny moment they found themselves in or observed with someone else. There's even a section of Hallmark cards featuring awkward family photos! Most often, they feature a family posing for a semi-professional shot back in the seventies or eighties—you know, the family photos with the blue backdrops that every grandmother has a copy of in her home somewhere. One of my personal favorites is the family that thought it would be cool if every single member, including both parents and all three children of various genders and ages, had matching shirts and mullet haircuts. Awkward indeed!

Well, finding spiritual family should not be awkward! It begins with making sure we are in the church body where God has placed us.

> *But as a matter of fact, God has placed each of the members in the body just as he decided*
> (I Corinthians 12:18 NET).

If we let Him, He will set us up to be, as our pastor says, "at the right place, at the right time, with the right people, doing the right things!" If God cares about a little bird that falls out of a tree, then surely we must believe that He knows how to guide us to our church family. But we must sincerely seek Him for that clear guidance and direction. Our church assignment is one of the most important determinations we will ever make. Our lives, even as families, should be centered around our own church. It's that important! Once this is in place, relationships can develop organically as we begin to relate to various genders and generations. Nothing awkward about that!

So you may say, "That all sounds good, but I'm still not sure who makes the first move in this potentially-awkward first dance. Do the spiritual children seek spiritual parents, or is it the other way around?" The short and easy answer is that either holds true. Let's back up for a minute. Once we have been placed in our church family by God, our next step is to pray and ask God to give us divine connections across generations, and for our hearts to be open to give and to receive from others. We must be open and willing both to lead and to be led. The world's culture says that we are to be independent of others. Society urges us to make our own decisions and to take care of ourselves first. In contrast, the culture of the Kingdom of God says that we are to be completely dependent on God and on others in His family. We are to put others first. He even says that we are to lay down our lives for others! We must have this truth settled in our hearts. Otherwise we won't see the need to pursue others or their wisdom and counsel. We will continue to live like most of the world, make lots of unnecessary mistakes, and completely miss out on the joy of life in community.

Once our heart is in the proper place, we can begin to avail ourselves of all the family and ministry contexts our church community has to offer. None of us will find spiritual family by just sitting in a church service hoping, day in and day out, to be pursued. Begin by becoming a full-fledged member of your church body. Does your church offer home groups, classes, discipling groups, Bible studies or gender-specific ministry groups that you could join? As a younger person, you don't just scan the church and pick a family you want to be a part of hoping that they, too, will receive you with open arms, warts and all! No, you trust the Lord to open doors and hearts, even in unexpected places. Besides, spiritual family seldom is just one person or one family. God will give you brothers and sisters, pastors and teachers, leaders in various capacities, mentors and friends, as well as spiritual moms and dads, all of whom may become your extended family in the Lord. You will have a team!

You may eventually have several spiritual moms and dads,

those older and more mature than you in the Lord, who will pour wisdom and counsel into the various seasons of your life. I have personally had dozens and dozens of young people refer to me as a spiritual mom. I have never asked any of them to call me that, but neither have I denied them that special title. I always feel privileged to be viewed in that manner, hoping always to steward their hearts in the ways of the Lord. To whatever degree it is possible, I see myself as a partner with their biological parents in helping nurture them in the Lord. As my pastor, Dale Evrist, says, "We can't raise your kids for you, but we can raise your kids with you." This is such a helpful perspective. All parents should understand this!

Unfortunately, many young adults in church today do not come from Christian homes where there is such a partnership available. Often, they are the only believer in their very dysfunctional, unstable family. It is those in particular, more so than all others, who need our help in navigating relationships of any kind. They especially need help in relating to and receiving from spiritual mentors and parents they can trust and lean into. In other words, we are addressing the way to approach potential ongoing, long-term mentoring and spiritual parenting relationships.

So let's get down to the nitty-gritty practicalities of how this works.

Who starts this process?

Either generation can approach the other to initiate. That changes later once a mentoring, spiritual parenting relationship is established. At that point it is primarily, but not exclusively, the role of the mentoree to pursue the leader in the relationship. Only when we are hungry to be spiritually led will we pursue those over us in the Lord. We will take responsibility to keep them current with what is going on in our lives and not expect that they will chase us down. At the same time, it is important to not inundate our mentors with every minor thought or issue that we face. We will discuss appropriate relational boundaries in Chapter Nine.

What do I say to pursue this connection?

Here is one example: An older person approaches a young person. "I would love to grab coffee with you sometime and hear more of your story."

Yes, it's that simple! Trust my years of experience: If you say those simple words, these young ones will feel pursued, loved, affirmed and valued. Never once have I been turned down or stood up. On the contrary; every single one has expressed genuine gratitude for the interest I have shown. More often than not, they almost always want to meet again. Most young people from dysfunctional family backgrounds find it hard to believe that anyone of another generation could be interested in them beyond a casual conversation.

That conversation may lead to something more formalized in

terms of connecting with them, or it may lead to connecting them with someone else who may be better suited to help them. Either way, you will have gotten to know them on a deeper level. You also will have modeled how to be a listener and an encourager! It's a win-win situation!

Here is an example of someone younger approaching an older person: "I would love to be able to connect with you over coffee sometime soon to get your counsel and input…on my entire life (just kidding!!) on a few things." Most of the time, a person will be deeply honored that you asked for their counsel and will work to get something scheduled.

Here's what not to say: "Will you be my Dad? First we can make snow angels for two hours, then we'll go ice skating, then we'll eat a whole role of cookie dough as fast as we can, and then to finish, we'll snuggle!" (It didn't go so well for Buddy The Elf, either. Ha!) You certainly don't want to overwhelm anyone with expectations or long-term commitments. This is where you must fully trust the Lord for His best.

You may feel a desire to connect with someone in particular, but it just never seems to work out. This may be because God has someone else in mind for you. Don't get discouraged! Look for the natural relationships that blossom from smaller group settings, such as men's or women's groups. Another way of reaching out is to meet with one of your pastors and ask them for help in connecting you with the right person. Once that initial connection happens, you'll be better able to discern whether or not that is God's chosen relational connection. If not, that initial meeting could serve to engage the help you need in finding the right fit. That way, you don't have to worry about putting someone on the spot if their plate is already full or the timing is just not right.

What do we talk about?

You start with getting to know each other better. If this is someone you have history with already, then this part isn't really necessary. However, if this is a fairly new relationship, you will need to gather a little history from each other for the sake of gaining perspective. Talk about where you grew up, briefly explore your family history and dynamics, share your personal testimony of how and when you came to Christ. Exchange your respective church experiences and what brought you to this church. This should only take about ten hours to complete. (Not really!) This first meeting should provide a general overview. Many of these topics may need to be covered in much greater depth at a later time. Nevertheless, if there is a pressing issue, that can certainly be brought up then. By the end of this first meeting, both of you should seek the Lord as to whether or not this connection is His chosen fit. If the Lord is confirming so, explore the possibility of meeting on a regular basis, perhaps at a fixed time.

At a recent fall party hosted by a family in our church, I met a newly-married young couple who moved into our community. As I was chatting with the wife, she mentioned that she had been to Bible college and wanted to be involved in ministry. I instantly offered to meet with her to hear her heart and story. She was excited I offered! I didn't know then whether this would be a one-time meeting or something more. As it turned out, I have begun meeting with her on a regular basis, and she has been so incredibly grateful. And it has been such a joy to get to spend time with her.

Each year I pray into which young women God would have me specifically mentor for the coming year or season. The Lord will usually highlight two or three young women, and I will approach them to share that the Lord has put them on my heart. I then typically offer to meet with them every other week for a given number of months. That way, we are both aware that we have an initial commitment on the front-end, but that does not entail the need to continue indefinitely. By setting these boundaries from the get-go, we can avoid needless hurt or rejection should the Lord redirect us. Short-term partnerships also give me the opportunity to connect with many different young ladies.

What is so beautiful about this process is the relationship that is developed over those months and sometimes years. Since I began to do this about fifteen years ago, some of these women have only really needed my input for that short season. Some simply call me Pastor Toni, some would call me a spiritual leader and friend, and others call me a spiritual mom, or just plain "Mom." Each relationship is unique and special in its own way. Each one fits perfectly as God desires.

When we are intentional about asking the Lord to open our heart to the next generation and purpose to pursue those relationships, we receive the benefits of really being in the family of God. And I have watched my husband pour his life into many young men in the same way! What blesses me beyond measure is now seeing most of the young women I have mentored pour their lives and hearts into other young women in similar fashion. This is truly my definition of "fruit that remains!"

Don't be afraid to have the DTR talk.

As I (Rachel) was growing up in California, it was very common for people to use the terminology "the DTR talk." This was especially true for people of a marriageable age. DTR stands for Define The Relationship. When members of the opposite sex were developing friendships, they would often have a conversation to define the context of their relationship in order to communicate their intentions clearly. It was basically a safeguard to make sure both parties of a relationship were on the same page. Expectations were understood, and the future of the relationship tracked with an agreed-upon destination.

Establishing spiritual family requires that we have a DTR talk. It might feel slightly awkward to have such an honest conversation about where the relationship may be heading, but it is essential to convey what you are sensing from the Lord as to His assignment. It is critical to stewarding one another well. When we begin to talk about family, we begin brushing up against very delicate places in people's hearts. Think about a courtship between a man and a woman, the season of engagement, all the preparations that go into a marriage, and how serious a covenant it is to create a new family. We can really guard one another's hearts by being willing to talk openly and gently about our expectations. We should define the level of commitment we pledge to each other. This holds true in a courtship, and it holds true in spiritual family.

It can be as simple as establishing how frequently you would like to connect with one another, for example. Should we only meet for coffee every other week? Should we sometimes have family dinner together with the rest of your family at your home? This can vary as the relationship progresses, and obviously, doesn't have to be determined right from the very beginning. However, be intentional about asking the Lord to show you when those points of clarification and communication need to happen.

My relationship with my spiritual mother progressed through various stages, and none of it was awkward. I was willing to ask questions about expectations just to be sure I was tracking with her appropriately. Her conversations with me gave me great training for the plethora of similar conversations I have had with my spiritual kids. So many times they have asked questions about what is normal or what is appropriate, and I have openly given them permission to do that. I know that family is where so many people are wounded. So if over-communicating is part of the healing process, bring it on! I want them to ask every time something new needs clarity. I know this is how biblical relating is learned and how wounds are uprooted. One conversation that may seem awkward to you can really help to ease the heart of another. It can bring great relief just to know where the boundaries and expectations should be placed.

What topics do we discuss after establishing ongoing mentoring/spiritual parenting?

Let me (Toni) first say that any good relationship is built on honesty and trust. Both people must be willing to be vulnerable and transparent. Although I have had spiritual kids bring along lists of things to discuss because they didn't want to forget something, these are not formal business meetings. They are Spirit-led conversations. So for those of you, like me, who happen to really appreciate lists, I will give you a list of potential topics you may want to cover.

- **Current life circumstances** – Talk about your week. Discuss anything significant or challenging. This is how we stay current and live life together in the Lord.

- **Spiritual disciplines** – How are you doing with the discipline of spending time in the Word and prayer? Be honest! This you should cover every time you meet. It is the foundation of our relationship both with God and with others. If we don't spend time pursuing the Lord, we will not gain ground relationally.

- **Spiritual insight** – Discuss any revelation and insight gained or sensed from the Holy Spirit that week. We need to be constantly growing in listening and hearing from the Lord.

- **Spiritual growth** – Discuss spiritual strengths and weaknesses to be developed. Are there areas needing breakthrough or deliverance?

- **Relational challenges** – Discuss primary relationships and healthy ways to navigate, improve or learn to set appropriate boundaries.

- **Work or school issues** – Both of these areas present challenges and opportunities for growth.

- **Finances** – Discuss financial issues including needs, strategies, and commitments to good stewardship.

- **Home/living situation** – A lot of young adults are in some type of temporary living situation, whether married or single, and need help navigating both the relational and physical dynamics of each circumstance.

- **Big life events** – Ok. Here we stop. This category requires its own sub-headings. Just like with biological kids, being a spiritual parent can place you in all kinds of transitions and seasons as the lives of your kids change. Here are some hints as to the big ones:

  * "So I'm interested in this guy…" = Marriage
  * "I would really like to buy a new car/home" = Major Purchases
  * "What kind of training do I need after high school?" = Education
  * "What am I supposed to do with my life?" = Vocational Calling
  * "Should I move to another city?" = Geographical Assignment

Relating to another generation by the Spirit is time-consuming. It can even seem overwhelming. But God has given each one of us a measure of grace to serve Him and to serve others for a lifetime. When we open ourselves up to others in the body of Christ, we never know what He will bring forth. We must remember that some relationships are meant for a season, some for a reason, and some for a lifetime. We don't begin by saying, "I want to be your spiritual mom," or, "I want to be your spiritual son." We begin by being open to relate to one another in intentional ways to provide and to receive from each other the wisdom and counsel needed to live our lives for our Heavenly Father. He is the only perfect parent. He generously invited us to be His very own children when we made Jesus Lord of our lives. Every relationship will be unique and different. What we seek is a God-ordained relationship with one of His children, a relationship that will please Him and will glorify and honor Him. He will lead it to the place He wants it to go.

We should make no assumptions except that we are committed to His process. For those more seasoned in the Lord, not every relationship will lead to spiritual parenting, even though every relationship is about spiritual family. All of us need every part of the Body of Christ. No one person carries it all. We may only carry one part, or God may give us a bigger role if a young person truly grows to view us as a spiritual parent. Even that means different things to different people. God is the one who makes the heart-connection and knows how to bring this all together. Some of our spiritual kids spend holidays and special occasions with us. Others don't because they don't need that from us. Each one has unique needs, and each connects differently with other spiritual and biological family members.

If someone you are mentoring comes from a broken home or has lost a parent, he or she may find great comfort in calling you "mom" or "dad." Others may use the term "spiritual mom" or "spiritual dad" as a way to honor the role you have held in their lives, even when they have great, spiritually-mature biological parents. Others may have given that special place to someone else but still really value you as a voice of wisdom and counsel in their life. The title is not the issue! The issue is that we give our lives freely to those the Lord is putting before us. There are no specific rules to follow. Where the Spirit of the Lord is, there is liberty. Just follow Jesus, first and foremost. Let Him lead in every single relationship. Don't try to make something fit just because you want it to. Submit everything to Him, and He will guide you through with peace and provision.

Prayer

Father in Heaven,

What an incredible privilege You have given us in finding spiritual family in the Church. Open our eyes to those who are divinely appointed to be in our lives in a more significant way. We want to find each other! We want to open our hearts to live transparently with those You have called us to partner with in life and ministry. We want to live in authentic community and to willingly parent and be parented by others as Your Spirit leads. Forgive us for selfish and self-centered living, for thinking that we are to live life on our own terms rather than receiving godly counsel about everything. Bring us together with our spiritual families and remove any obstacles that would stand in our way. We thank You that family is Your idea and ideal, and that You have made provision in Your household for each of us. We want to embrace and receive Your love for us and through us as we reach out to another generation in great faith in the days to come.

In Jesus' name, Amen!

Eight

Beware, It's Messy! Part 1

The Granddaddy of Them All

Last night, after Easter supper, we sat around the table in my spiritual grandma's kitchen eating dessert and talking about silly stuff like her seventy-five-year-old perspective on selfies and Facebook. We laughed and laughed…and laughed. It was just us girls, four generations to be exact. There was my spiritual nana, Toni's mom, my spiritual mom, Toni, two of my spiritual daughters, and me (Rachel). It was one of those precious moments in life that feel so perfect you can't script or plan for it. You just realize it is happening and hope your heart drinks enough of it in to remember the sweetness of it for years to come. In the midst of the laughter, Nana shared about how she is believing for the Lord to heal her body from its painful battle with arthritis. Immediately, without hesitation, we all stopped and gathered around her to pray. She started the prayer time by giving thanks to God for all the faithfulness of over sixty years of walking closely with Him. Undergirding her every syllable was an overwhelming sense of gratitude. Then I listened as Toni prayed with faith-filled petitions to her Heavenly Father that were saturated in obvious love and compassion for her mother. After I had a chance to pray for Nana, my heart got stuck in my throat just a little, as I listened to my spiritual daughters add their great prayers of faith, compassion and love. These moments are a precious gift. They make all the moments that seem like such hard work so very worth it all. I think my spiritual mom would say the same thing about all the hard work she has poured into me as well; she, too, would count it all joy!

None of us are perfect. Not a single one of us. We all have wounds, quirks, and a life full of experiences that we carry into any given situation. Have you ever accidentally cut your hand with a knife? Have you noticed the healing that occurs over the weeks that follow? Better yet, have you ever seen a skin graft, how one part of a person's body is used to reconstruct another, a part that desperately needed healing? Our very bodies are designed to heal themselves. Isn't that miraculous? Our bodies are meant to heal themselves!

This is also true for the Body of Christ. The Body is equipped to bring healing to itself. When you bring a broken or wounded follower of Christ into a healthy, functioning church, healing will take place. If everyone is actively engaging the way they were meant to, just as a body functions in the way it was meant to, healing will occur. The miraculous healing power of the Holy Spirit will breathe health into anyone who is willing to receive it. The body of believers should be willing to participate in that process. God does the healing. We just have to participate.

Let's keep this truth in mind as we look at the rest of the components of this chapter. We are going to talk about the potential relational barriers and areas of wounding that may be encountered as you journey towards becoming spiritual family. This list is not meant to be exhaustive, rather it delineates the most common hurdles that can challenge us. Please, don't be intimidated. Be encouraged. God wants to move in the area of healing and freedom. We get to be a part of what HE will do if we are willing. If you recognize these traits within yourself, don't be embarrassed or shrink back. Remember, these are the most *common* hurdles we have encountered and also the areas in which we have most commonly seen the Lord move mightily.

Rejection and Shame

Let's start with the granddaddy of them all: Rejection and its twin sister, Shame. Both of these are heavy-hitters in their capacity to damage and impact the heart and soul of a person. This close relationship between rejection and shame is rooted in the fact that they both launch an arrow right at the core of someone's sense of worth. Now, when we talk about rejection here, we aren't talking about it from the surface-life level that we all inevitably face. We are talking about those who have been wounded at a foundational level of their personhood.

To reject someone is to push them away. To reject is to

refuse, to turn away from, to discard, to refuse to believe in, to refuse to receive, embrace, or sometimes even to love. Experiencing deep rejection can lead people into the bondage of shame. Shame comes not from the sense of healthy conviction over a sin committed, but from a belief system founded on the understanding that there is something wrong with who you are as a person.

This is not always, but quite often, a scheme of the Enemy. It comes into a person's life with great force at moments of trauma. There is a spiritual assault that happens at the same time that a physical or sexual abuse takes place. It can come in with great damaging power in areas of abandonment. Look with eyes of compassion and discernment, and try to imagine all the demonic assaults that might try to come against the little girl in this scenario:

> *I recall a young woman telling me about the day she and her sibling came home from school when they were ten and eight to find their mother there with a suitcase packed for each of them. With no warning as to the coming situation, their mother decided it was time for them to go live with their father (undoubtedly, those children would have already felt the sting of abandonment). She immediately took them to the airport and waved goodbye as they were given no choice but to get on the plane to go to another state and live with their father. They would discover, after they arrived, that he was heavily addicted to methamphetamines. He had checked out completely,*

both mentally and emotionally.

Can you begin to imagine how that might have felt? The Enemy looks for prime opportunities such as these to capitalize on the emotional turmoil that is happening in order to implant lies that cause further pain. These are lies that he will inevitably try to reinforce at every turn in the hope of enslaving us. They become strongholds of bondage in a person's life.

Being bound by rejection and shame is kind of like wearing a pair of glasses and a set of earmuffs that constantly filter everything you see and hear through a fixed suggestion. That suggestion convinces us that those we relate to have underlying motives to disregard us or to distance themselves from us. It is a dreadful lie and an incredibly painful way to live. That false reality presumes that something is wrong with us, that we are shamful and unworthy, and that we cannot be partakers of intimacy that lasts because our personhood is fundamentally flawed. It robs the person of the peace God intended for relationship. The love, joy, acceptance, and embrace of the Holy Spirit, an embrace that comes from godly relationships, cannot be received under these circumstances.

Furthermore, these warping glasses often become magnifiers. In the realm of human relationships with imperfect people, that warped perception becomes active and places obstacles in the way of building trust and healthy attachment. This causes great pain. Spiritual parents who have poured out their love richly and freely feel it too. It can seem as though no matter how much they give, it doesn't ever seem to be enough. Both parties can feel stuck. This trap can only be overcome by pressing through consistently. Even in the face of disappointment, love, affirmation, and assurance must prevail.

To spiritual parents we advise this: remain steady. Be who you are in the Lord. Your spiritual kids will either receive you for who you are, or they will try to find someone else who they think may be a better fit. Do not grow weary. Remember, those young people are struggling! Sadly, depending on the spiritual maturity and receptivity of those we serve, this pattern can repeat itself many times. Either way, know that you have loved well and have given them a chance to fully receive from the Lord. It is important to be aware of this so when it happens, you will know how to press on. These wounded ones need that. Our security becomes part of the process of healing as they work through their pain. We should note that no one ever experienced rejection the way Jesus did. He knows how to heal even the deepest wounds. If we let Him, He will use His body, the Church, to accomplish just that.

Obviously, this process happens with people in varying degrees. It isn't always this heavy, intense encounter. Sometimes it is subtle and barely even noticed. Ask the Lord for discernment and wisdom. He will help you to identify when this scheme of the Enemy is at work. Only then can you be effective in ministering freedom whenever you find the opportunity. Once you are aware of this, you may be surprised at how often you can recognize these patterns in someone's life. We should never judge, condemn, or disregard someone's pain. When we recognize rejection issues, let's ask the Lord to help us discern what is happening, and what is causing the torment of those being affected so that we, moved with compassion, can pray and contend for their freedom.

If you are relating to someone who struggles with rejection and shame, compassion, wisdom, and prayer will always serve you well, whether or not you are a spiritual parent. As a spiritual parent, you have even greater access to offer love and godly counsel. Through these situations, the Lord will manifest healing in the life of the wounded. As His Body seeks to function as that agent of healing, it will serve to heal its own. Our healthy dynamics bring healing to the Body of Christ. As often as you are given access and opportunity, help every person to see the unhealthy trends in their life. Pray with them. Ask the Lord to reveal where wounds may be rooted, and contend, in the Spirit, for healing and restoration. Minister His compassion, mercy and power. It doesn't have to become overwhelming! The Holy Spirit alone brings healing and deliverance. Be encouraged. Never underestimate the healing power you carry into any situation by offering acceptance, love, and timely-spoken words of truth and consistency. This communicates that a person is wanted and gives them a chance to feel like they belong.

If you are a spiritual son or daughter who struggles in this area, be encouraged! There is great hope for freedom. This has probably been one of the greatest struggles I have faced and one of the greatest avenues to my deliverance and victory. I have seen the trenches of darkness, of deep pain that causes damage, and also the height of love the Lord is willing to go to in order to bring those He loves out of bondage.

> *And they overcame him by the blood of the Lamb and by the word of their testimony, and they did not love their lives to the death* (Revelation 12:11).

I am going to be vulnerable, now, and share a part of my testimony, in the hope that it will give you the courage to overcome.

It had been quite a while since I had embraced this beautiful revelation of spiritual family. I was feeling much more confident about belonging to a church family. I knew I had heard the direction of the Lord clearly in moving to Tennessee. I was finishing my second year of a student intern training program for pastoral ministry while working on finishing my Master's Degree in Pastoral Counseling. So many relational dynamics had become my comfort during those two years, and they were a huge part of the structure that God had set in place for that season. I had been immersed in education. And that season was about to come to a close.

Those previous two years, I had worked so hard to come to freedom in the Lord. Countless prayers had been prayed, and innumerable actions of obedient faith had taken place despite my fears. I had been at war in the spirit to see the bondage of rejection and shame broken off of my life and replaced with the truth written in God's Word. Others, too, had completely engaged in contending for my breakthrough. I knew I was safe. I knew none of the people I loved were going anywhere. I knew, that I knew, that I knew, that the Lord loved me. I was exactly where I was supposed to be.

But change hung in the air. I could feel those old familiar places triggering. Fear began to rise within. I sat in the parking lot of the church with Toni after we had gotten back from our mentoring time. We had talked about the future and all the great things the Lord had in store. Suddenly, tears unexpectedly flooded my eyes.

"What's going to happen now?" I asked her.

"What do you mean?" she said.

"Now that I am graduating and everything is changing, I feel so insecure about so many of my relationships."

She smiled compassionately, and in that most familiar, peaceful tone she said, "Be at peace. Now we just do life together."

I realized that I hadn't grasped that part of it yet. I had come from such a background of rejection, abandonment, and shame, that I didn't have a context to help me understand how to do life outside the structure of serving and performing. It hit me like a punch in the gut and opened the door for the Lord to lead me to a whole new realm of healing. I was being given the opportunity to shake off a mentality that I didn't even realize I had. I had been functioning as someone who believed that I could only be welcomed into relationship if, somehow, I could be useful. Doesn't that sound like the mentality of one who's been marked with shame and rejection? That was me. On the other side of that "just-got-punched-in-the-gut" feeling, that feeling that happens when rejection gets triggered, is a beautiful, wonderful, amazing freedom! That is good news! It's there for us every time if we are willing to grab hold of it.

The Lord showed me that even though I had embraced family, I was still functioning under a mentality of "works." I had yet to fully understand grace. The law tells us that we have to perform. We must serve and be useful in order to be accepted and invited into relationship. Grace tells us that we already belong, and because we belong, we offer acts of love and service. One posture serves to obtain love. The other serves from having received love. The first mindset is that of a servant, while the other is the mindset of a true son or a daughter. I hadn't realized I was still functioning under the law with the mindset of a servant. I felt so much freedom just from being loved and accepted. I had no capacity to understand that there was so much MORE!

The spirit of adoption within God's heart doesn't want a house full of slaves. He wants sons and daughters! He doesn't want us to serve Him to earn a small token of His love. He wants us to know beyond a shadow of a doubt how very loved we are, and it is that love that compels us towards serving Him. This is the very heart of spiritual family. I was still learning this.

I have come to see that the wounds and damaging mindsets that result from the sting of rejection are often healed in layers. I know that's not the best news you've heard today. But honestly, there's mercy in it. I remember crying out to God in frustration over the level of detailed work it took for me to gain freedom in this area of my life. I was desperate to be free once and for all. I wanted never to deal with this again. I'll never forget the picture God dropped into my mind and spirit in response to that cry of desperation. He showed me an image of a silhouette of the first time my step-father ever came into our room seeking to sexually abuse me and my older sister. Then He showed me a snapshot, in the spirit, of the number of demonic spirits that were there, working through my stepfather for their own agenda. One devastating moment of someone's sinful act can greatly damage the spirit of a person.

Then the Lord said to me, *"Rachel, I am thankful for your willingness to allow Me to bring healing and freedom from some of these demonic assaults against your life, but I am not willing to allow that any of them remain. My heart is for you to receive the full measure of healing that the Cross affords. Don't you want ALL I have for you?"*

Of course, I said yes! Who am I to be impatient when the God of the universe is seeking to bring me total freedom from the places that have scarred my life, denying me access to His heavenly agenda?

God is a healer. His heart is to liberate, to deliver, and to gently heal our broken hearts.

> *He has sent Me to heal the brokenhearted, to proclaim liberty to the captives, and the opening of the prison to those who are bound* (Isaiah 61:1).

He is the One who heals. That is who He is! Relational wounds can be so deeply rooted. It takes the skillful hand of a merciful surgeon to remove them without causing further damage. It takes the Holy Spirit. He knows what He is doing. He is patient. His timing is perfect. His methods are flawless. Best of all, His intentions and motives are pure love and absolute compassion.

So I say to you, sweet child of God, you who may be suffering from the pain and wounds of rejection and shame, God sees you. He sees all of who you are, and He declares you worthy. You are worthy of His love because He declares you to be. He assigns your value regardless of your understanding of what you're worth. He loves you with a love beyond measure. He has called you His own and declares you to be the apple of His eye, the very center of His focus. He promises you the full measure of your healing. He has already paid for it on the Cross. His freedom is yours if you will allow Him to execute His good plan.

Your role is to lean. Lean into what He is doing. Whom is He asking you to trust? Where is He asking you to let your guard down? What walls must come down in order for love and healing to flow? Trust Him. Before you trust any other person on the planet, trust Him. After all, He made the planet, and He made you! He is trustworthy! Believe Him to bring healing. Read and study His Word. Meditate on His promises and truth that you may grow in faith, knowing that freedom will come. It is assured! His truth will set you free. It is your hope, your promise and the pledge He's written in His Word.

Having done this, offer to trust your spiritual family. They are the ones He has provided for your healing. When God brings us into spiritual family, we can trust Him to shepherd us through the process. Trust and love the spiritual family you are blessed to be part of, even when they make mistakes. They are God's gift, His blessing. God's grace is big enough to cover their mistakes, too. They are human. They will make mistakes and need permission to be human. If you have a standard of perfection they must live up to, you will be continuously disappointed and isolated. Human relationships are flawed because humans are flawed. Nevertheless, when our heart motives are right and in alignment with the Lord, His grace and shepherding will lead us all through together. On the other side are green pastures and still waters. On the other side there is peace, and love, and a safe place to belong. It's all so worth it.

This is not, by any means, a comprehensive guide through all the complexities of rejection and shame. These topics alone can take up an entire book. But please, do be encouraged in this: When we are willing to rest in the loving arms of our Heavenly Father, regardless of the depth of our pain, good things will come. We can't go wrong in journeying towards Him. His heart will lead us. We mustn't underestimate the power of prayer. This is how we are changed. In prayer, in the Word, in His presence, in the midst of His loving embrace, we are healed. This we know, absolutely, positively, completely, without a single doubt: You are loved.

We encourage you to pray this beautiful prayer from Ephesians 3. Pray it out loud, letting the sound of your voice be heard in the heavenlies:

Prayer

Father, the Creator of everything in heaven and on earth,

I pray that from Your glorious, unlimited resources, You will empower me with inner strength through Your Spirit. I ask that You, Christ, will make Your home in my heart, as I trust in You. Help me to trust You! I pray that my roots will grow deep down into Your love. God, keep me strong. Grant me the power to understand, as all Your people should, how wide, how long, how high, and how deep Your love is. May I experience the love of Christ, though it is too great to fully understand. Only then, I will be made complete with all the fullness of life and power that comes from You, God.

Amen.

(Ephesians 3:14-19)

Nine

Beware, It's Messy! Part 2
Other Tricky Little Boogers

In addition to the granddaddy of relational barriers posed by rejection and shame, there are several potentially-tricky obstacles that we should explore. In identifying these, we will further equip you to navigate successfully.

Unhealed Wounds

Have you ever come into direct contact with someone's blatant display of bitterness? Has the unpleasant fragrance of unforgiveness reached your nose? Whether in your own life or in that of another, bitterness and unforgiveness are ugly. They are evident in criticism, judgment, accusation, complaining and cynicism. Underneath them lie anger, rebellion, and stubbornness, which are often indicative of wounds that have yet to be fully healed. These relational barriers are telling. They serve as indicators that a greater work still needs to happen within one's soul. Often these souls need to lament before the Lord, to walk through repentance, to offer forgiveness, and to break agreement with demonic activity.

As spiritual parents, you need to be equipped. First, pray for the Lord to grant you wisdom, revelation, and discernment. Ask the Holy Spirit for insight into the hearts of your children in the faith. Don't be reactive, and remember that their hurtful actions stem from unhealed wounds. Don't be afraid to expose the patterns you see. After all, most of those who look for spiritual parents need and desire this very input. Our discernment helps them grow and mature in the spirit.

It is very common for young people to come into the context of the Church from broken families. Many of these young men and women carry deep relational wounds from their family of origin. We can't even begin to count the number of times we've encountered this. Over and over, we see these young people suddenly respond to us in a way that seems out of proportion to the situation at hand. Soon we discover that they are projecting the hurt they've experienced with their biological families. Once this is uncovered, we've been able to help them heal in Christ and to be able to forgive their parents. Quite often, we've seen great fruit develop in the relationship between our spiritual kids and their biological parents. That fruit has been the result of them being enabled by God to release their bitterness and to find healing of past hurts. Ultimately, the goal is to help them remove any hindrance, regardless of what relationship or situation invited it into being, that could block them from fully receiving God's love.

If you find yourself in that situation, if you have unhealed wounds that you may or may not have recognized, you should pray and seek the Lord. Ask Him to grant you wisdom, revelation, and discernment about what is happening in your heart, mind and emotions. Our emotions and thoughts will reveal the root cause of our pain. If you find yourself steeped in bitterness, anger, or rebellion, or if you find yourself projecting negative emotions onto your spiritual parents, ask yourself the question, "Is this really about them?" Be very careful not to regress into behaving like a child. And don't expect your spiritual parents to respond as though you have the responsibility level of a ten-year-old. Even though your role is that of a spiritual son or daughter, you are still an adult. As such, you should conduct yourself in like manner. That's a little golden nugget, a friendly "hug of wisdom," if you will, to help you avoid embarrassing situations!

Are there areas of further healing you may need the Lord to highlight in your life? Do you experience pain or soul wounds that you have yet to lay at the feet of your Heavenly Father? Have you fully received His love and healing? Do you need to forgive and release members of your family from past hurts and offenses? Do you have areas where you need to repent? Do you need to examine whether you have bitterness towards God, the Father? Could it be that you may be projecting that bitterness onto those who occupy roles of authority? There are so many areas that can trip us up in relational dynamics. But bitterness that leads to unforgiveness is a doozy! It will continue to cause relational damage in every area of life if you leave it unchecked. Ask the Holy Spirit to highlight the source. What is causing the pain in your heart? He will be so faithful. Give Him the opportunity. His heart is one of compassion. He longs to heal. Things like unforgiveness and bitterness, unattended wounds, and childhood trauma limit our capacity to receive the fullness of God's mercy.

The gospels are filled with accounts of Jesus being moved with compassion on behalf the broken and bound. Compassion was the chief motivation behind His miracles. Hebrews 13:8 tells us that,

> *"Jesus Christ is the same yesterday today and forever."*

That means that He still desires to move in compassion to bring a miracle of healing into your life. Did you know that the very fact that you can exchange your hurt for His mercy is itself a miracle? Through His forgiveness, we can be healed. Forgiveness and repentance are absolute gifts from the God of love. They usher in the miracle of healing. If we will embrace, celebrate, and employ them often, we will experience more freedom than we ever imagined.

Unmet Needs

Another area of relational hindrance comes in the form of unmet needs. After about three days with no water, the human body will perish. Hydration is a need. We were all created with basic needs. Every human being needs these fundamental things:

- Sustenance – air, sleep, food, water, shelter, clothing
- Safety – care, protection
- Relationship – community, belonging, family, connectedness
- Identity – value, worth
- Purpose – role, responsibility, direction

Generally speaking, most of us are adequately taken care of in the area of sustenance. Few of us would be reading this book if we were naked, starving, or had no place to sleep tonight. If someone knocked at our door and was naked and starving, I can't imagine any of us would not hurry to find some clothes and a warm meal for the poor soul.

The other four categories of basic human needs are just as essential to our well-being. They are not physical but emotional needs. If we had eyes that could see through a person into their spirit and soul, we would understand the reality of those needs. Just like we'd respond to the sad, naked person at our door, we would respond to each other with that same level of self-sacrifice and love.

These emotional needs are legitimate. They are God-given needs within the soul of every person. When these go unmet in the way the Creator intended them to be met, they often end up being met in an illegitimate manner. Children in developing nations who are without clean drinking water will end up drinking whatever kind of water they find, no matter how dirty. As a result, they will become very ill. This is an example, in the physical, of what happens to the soul when basic needs go unmet. When legitimate needs of the human soul are not met in legitimate ways, the Enemy sneaks in. He provides counterfeit options for meeting those needs in illegitimate ways. This is how most addictions start. Relational and substance addictions stem from unmet needs.

Co-dependency, unhealthy soul ties, unrealistic relational expectations, fears, and so many other behavioral issues come from the same root: unmet, legitimate needs. It isn't very tempting for someone whose belly is full of good, nutritious food to make a pit-stop at a fast food drive-through. There's no need to hit the grease pit. Why? Because there is no hunger. The belly is full. There is no appeal for the unhealthy things the world offers. Obviously, not every addiction or relational problem has the same source. However, it is certainly the source of many of them. Our souls are meant to be full of the healthy, life-giving presence of the Holy Spirit.

Because this is area is similar to that of unhealed wounds, much of the counsel given earlier in this chapter applies here as well. So many times the gaping hole of an unmet need will be detected by emotional triggers or behavioral patterns. We simply need to know how to respond to those triggers, identifying their source readily.

As a spiritual son or daughter, when you feel emotional triggers, ask the Lord to reveal their root. Talk to your spiritual parents about what the Lord is showing you. Ask them to partner with you in prayer, and together, contend for restoration. Seek God's fulfillment, and genuine health. Be proactive. Voice your needs to the Lord, and seek counsel from the Holy Spirit. Engage your spiritual parents and leaders as to how to get those needs legitimately met. God didn't create your soul with needs with the intent to leave you wanting and empty. He has a plan for legitimate satisfaction.

He wants us full!

For those of you who mentor, if you are witnessing behavioral patterns that concern you, ask the Lord to give you discernment. Ask Him if there are unmet needs in the lives of your spiritual kids. Seek revelation to know the root issue beneath the surface. Ask Him to show you what His plan is and to lead you in the specific ways He'd have you partner with Him in leading your spiritual children to restoration. How can you usher them to the Source of all fullness, the Holy Spirit, and into community?

I have personally sat across from many, many heartbroken, empty young women. They have gone without, not knowing how to have their emotional needs met for so long. That has led them to dreadful confusion and even to disorientation about their sexuality and identity. Cloaked in shame and blinded, these sweet girls, daughters of the Most High God, had yet to realize that He doesn't shame their needs. Those needs are legitimate. He wants them to be met in healthy ways to overflowing!

The Enemy of our soul will always exploit the areas where we lack understanding. He will always seek to gain territory. The Lord values our soul, our mind, emotions, and our spirit above all things. He created every aspect of us! He created us with needs on purpose. They aren't accidental and shouldn't be ignored. Becoming whole requires us to give attention to these areas. It is a worthy endeavor to understand our needs. That discovery becomes the most beautiful place of our communion with God. It is a place overflowing with His love.

Humility and Entitlement

We talked a little bit in Chapter Six about honor. We are called to honor our spiritual parents with the same love and devotion that God requires towards our biological mothers and fathers. Honor is so closely tied to humility.

> *The fear of the Lord is the instruction of wisdom, and before honor is humility* (Proverbs 15:33).

It is only by walking in humility that we are spiritually prepared to receive honor. Through our willingness and obedience to walk the humble walk, we become better poised to bestow honor on others.

Humility is an essential component for every relationship to function in thriving health. This couldn't be any more true than within the dynamics of spiritual family. When everyone walks humbly, that posture provides the greatest possible opportunity for the Holy Spirit to move as He brings redemption. In order to have our hearts truly knit to one-another in lasting bonds, we must become humble. Humility prepares an incredible canvas for the Lord. Upon it, He creates the most beautiful masterpiece of family.

The opposite of this, one of the nastiest little boogers of the soul, is entitlement. It is so ugly and is unfortunately prevalent in our society and this generation. It rears its head in the most unsuspecting places. Basically, entitlement is the false notion that a person has a right to something devoid of any responsibility whatsoever. It is a perceived right without a perceived responsibility. It asks, "What are you going to do for me?" It never asks, "What can I do for you?" One should expect that from an appropriately dependent toddler but not from a grown adult. That posture is unacceptable among grown-ups.

Relationships work two ways. If we want to have spiritual sons and daughters, we must become spiritual parents. If we want to have spiritual parents, we must become spiritual sons and daughters. Humility is key. Both parties must shoulder the responsibility of making the relationship work. If everyone is asking the Lord to show them how to serve, honor and love one another, the relationship will thrive. Entitlement is selfishness. Selfishness is the number one, quickest, most effective way to slaughter any relationship. Just don't do it! Don't feel entitled. Don't be afraid to confront it when you see it. It must be arrested. It cannot rear its ugly head.

Boundaries

Dr. Henry Cloud and Dr. John Townsend wrote a book entitled *Boundaries*. In it, they explain that, "Any confusion of responsibility and ownership in our lives is a problem of boundaries...we need to set mental, physical, emotional, and spiritual boundaries for our lives to help us distinguish what is our responsibility and what isn't." Boundaries are important in every relationship. Spiritual family is no exception. Navigating through and setting healthy boundaries can be tricky at times. Since most of us haven't grown up in homes where that was modeled, we don't have a frame of reference for how this should look.

The Scriptures have much to say on this topic. Most of us are familiar with the idea of carrying one another's burdens. Rightly so, Galatians teaches us that it is how we model Christianity.

> *Carry each other's burdens and in this way fulfill the law of Christ* (Galatians 6:2).

However, it's important to note that the emphasis is on "each other's." Each of us must learn about and own our individual responsibility. Boundaries have to do with taking personal responsibility. We have responsibilities even when receiving counsel and care from others.

> *Each one should carry his own load* (Galatians 6:5).

Despite our understanding that we should help carry one another's burdens, we are nevertheless responsible for our own load. How does this principle relate to spiritual family? Here are some tips.

Coaching Notes for Spiritual Parents:

- Cultivate a deep relationship with the Lord, then help your spiritual kids do the same.

- Always, always direct those you lead to first seek answers from Jesus through prayer and the Word. Your first priority is to strengthen their relationship with God. There should be no unhealthy dependence upon you. Also, once they have prayed about an issue and sought your counsel, direct them to other reliable voices in their lives.

Where there is no counsel, the people fall; but in the multitude of counselors there is safety
(Proverbs 11:14).

- Model appropriate relational boundaries in your own life. It's ok to let them know that you have personal boundaries with your time.

- Allow spiritual kids to take responsibility for their own choices.

- Don't constantly rescue them from the consequences of poor choices.

- Don't tell them what to do unless there is biblical sin or disobedience going on. Avoid the sin of control. Do not seek to control others' actions even for righteous motives. God has given us a free will to choose. We must do the same for one another.

- Teach spiritual children to have appropriate boundaries and to respect the boundaries of others.

Coaching Notes for Spiritual Kids:

- Don't expect anyone but Jesus to be your personal Savior. Spiritual family is God's provision, but He is the source!

- Don't blow up their phone! Multiple text messages, phone calls, emails, etc., on a daily basis is overwhelming. Be respectful of their time and boundaries. The goal is to be a blessing to them, even as they are to you.

- Take responsibility for your feelings, behaviors, choices and thoughts. Don't blame others!

- Don't hold spiritual parents responsible for your emotions. You are a steward of your own vessel and emotions. No one else can be responsible for your emotions, since no one else has direct control over them like you do.

- Agree when the truth exposes issues in your life. Receive godly counsel with grace.

- Develop appropriate, relational boundaries with others in your life according to God's Word. Learn when to say yes and when to say no!

- Never violate your conscience.

- Never make others feel guilty for their personal boundaries. Do not feel guilt about yours.

- Take personal responsibility for your life in Christ!

Maintaining appropriate boundaries is a great way to strengthen relationships. Knowing what lies within the realm of your responsibility versus someone else's is a huge key to growing in relational maturity. If you have questions about where those boundaries lie, ask! Grasping this understanding and walking it out wholeheartedly not only strengthens your relationships, it also keeps your heart well-guarded.

Prayer

Lord Jesus,

We pray that You would grant us great wisdom as we navigate through these priceless relationships. Grant us the mind of Christ so that we may be vessels of honor as we relate to one another. Let our hearts be tender and receptive to Your truth, Your compassion, Your love, and Your care. As we receive these things, let us give of them generously. Help us to be patient with one another as we journey into new territory together. We surrender to Your guidance and ask that You would lead us into healthy relationships with one another, relationships that reflect Your love and Your light to the world around us.

In Jesus' mighty name,

Amen!

Ten

Truly Fruitful

Remember those classic word problems in school? They usually went something like this: Four children have small toys. The first child has one tenth of the toys. The second child has twelve more toys than the first. The third child has one more toy than the first child has, and the fourth child has double the third child. How many toys are there in all? Just reading this problem makes me want to cry! First of all, I (Toni) don't even understand the question. I can't imagine how long it would take me to figure it out. Furthermore, I don't even care what the answer is and have no motivation to work my "word-based" brain this hard. On the other hand, my husband, who majored in Structural Engineering, can be found working these types of problems for fun.

Isn't it funny how most people are either good with words or good with numbers? When we think about the Kingdom of God, we most often think about the words that need to be spoken and the words that need to be read and applied; but the gospel is also about numbers. Now I'm not talking about how many people attend your church. I'm talking about how many people in your church are bearing fruit for the Kingdom of God and multiplying the life of Christ into others. In Genesis 1:28 and 9:7, God told Adam and then Noah to be fruitful and multiply, to bring forth offspring abundantly in the earth and multiply in it. God told Noah that He would establish His covenant with him and his descendants after him. Neither one of these men could do this alone, so God created partnership with women to fully reflect His image of community.

Larry Christenson, a contributor to the Spirit-Filled Life Bible says, "When God chose to create man in His own image, He created marriage, He created a family. The community of the family is a reflection of the community in the Godhead. Its identity, life, and power come from God." It should not surprise us that Satan works so hard to destroy marriages and families. He wants to destroy the image of God and thwart its reproduction wherever possible. He's happy (if that's even possible) when couples live together instead of get married. If they do get married, his strategy is the destruction of that family. It delights him all the more to distort God's image and have two people of the same sex be attracted to each other, because they have no capacity to multiply, and they create an incomplete and perverted image of God. God's Word is clear from the very beginning in the Garden of Eden that family is meant to come from one man and one woman.

Family is about husbands and wives, sons and daughters, fathers and mothers multiplying themselves generation after generation. It is not simply reproducing human beings but reproducing the life and power of God in the next generation. The very essence of multiplication within the Kingdom is bringing sons and daughters into the family of God by sharing the gospel with them, leading them to Christ, and discipling them to maturity. From their maturity, they sow into the lives of others, thus multiplying God's Kingdom even further. As a spiritual parent, my role involves not only being an available and loving mentor to help sons and daughters navigate life's personal challenges, but to see them become mature in Christ and, in turn, make me a spiritual grandparent.

This is not about age but about stage. It's about a heart and mindset to pour into the next generation. I have seen young adults in their twenties parenting middle-schoolers and high-schoolers within the context of the Church, and thirty-year-olds parenting those in their twenties by spending time with them, loving on them and praying for their growth and freedom in Christ. However, the greatest need seems to be among our twenty- to thirty-years-olds. They need someone of an older, wiser generation to come alongside them and help them navigate life. Many, if not most, of them have come to Christ in spite of unspeakable pain, loss, and even abusive backgrounds. They haven't grown up in strong Christian families who nurtured them in the ways of the Lord. Some of them don't have a family at all. Find someone who is hungry for the Lord and less mature in Christ than you, and begin to pour into them all that's been poured into you. That's what it really means to be fruitful and multiply!

I began mentoring Rachel when she was about thirty years old and single. Within three or four years, she began to see herself as a spiritual mom to several younger women in our church body who were very drawn to her. God has brought many young men and women into our church body who come from very unstable family backgrounds similar to Rachel's. God sent Rachel to us, as well as many others like her, to help establish these lost young souls in His family. He wants them to find in Him what they thought they could never have.

Our church is filled with person after person, couple after couple, who have given themselves over to parenting the next generation. Many of our families have had younger singles live with them for a period of time while they partnered with others as spiritual family. Our founding pastor, Dale Evrist, has instilled this into our church DNA from the very beginning of our church plant. He and his wife, Joan, have been models and advocates of creating context for community and family. They believe in the importance of community for the believer from the core of their being and are committed to raising up and releasing the next generation with no gender bias whatsoever. I believe that, because our church has embraced this model of deeply caring for the relationally broken, we have been entrusted with some of God's most precious jewels.

I want to transition and allow Rachel to share her process from being a broken young woman in need of spiritual parents to so quickly becoming a spiritual mother herself. Rachel is an example of the sweet fruit that comes from embracing spiritual family even when it feels painful, risky, and vulnerable. She has multiplied all that has been poured into her and carries the truths and impartation she has received with conviction and passion everywhere she goes. She is a true daughter in every sense of the word. She treats my husband, Kevin, and me with more love and honor than we could have ever imagined. She was and continues to be a gift from God to us and to our church family. I can't think of a greater example of God's redemption in someone's life. He truly makes all things new, bringing life where there is none at all. She gets it! I pray that as you are reading this, you will open your heart to believe that God can redeem anything that you are willing to submit to Him and the process of redemption.

What a treasure to my (Rachel's) heart to hear my spiritual parents talk about me being a blessing to them. I truly feel like I am on the other side of a Cinderella story. I wish I could take a snapshot of my life now and show it to the desperate, broken, and scared version of myself as I was driving across the country to move to Nashville almost a decade ago. Then again, the journey wouldn't have required much faith. This truly has been a journey of faith and blessing—not always easy but always worth it.

That younger version of me probably wouldn't have believed that snapshot, as even now I often find myself in awe and wonder of all the Lord has done. He is magnificent, faithful, and a greater storyteller than any man who has ever lived. Who else would have looked at me and seen possibility and promise? Who else would have seen me in my darkest moments and rescued me with these new moments in mind? He is a Mighty God, the Father of all fathers. He lit the path in front of me one step at a time and said, "Walk here, then here," until He led me fully through. I have heard this passage of Scripture read at funerals, but to me, it is my song of victory. It is the song of my soul, which grabbed ahold of the hand of the Great Shepherd, and learned firsthand of His goodness and mercy.

> *The LORD is my shepherd; I shall not want. He makes me to lie down in green pastures; He leads me beside the still waters. He restores my soul; He leads me in the paths of righteousness for His name's sake.*
>
> *Yea, though I walk through the valley of the shadow of death, I will fear no evil; for YOU are with me; Your rod and Your staff, they comfort me.*
>
> *You prepare a table before me in the presence of my enemies; You anoint my head with oil; my cup runs over. Surely goodness and mercy shall follow me all the days of my life; and I will dwell in the house of the LORD forever* (Psalm 23).

My cup runs over.

When the topics of spiritual family, redemption, or the heart of the Lord towards family comes up, this is my immediate thought: My cup runs over. My heart is overflowing with gratitude, is blessed beyond measure and ready to spill His goodness upon anyone who wants to share in it.

I grew up with the heart of an orphan. I was raised by parents who did the best they could but who were bound in darkness and overrun with evil. I came as close to death as a person can come without actually dying. I was well acquainted with hopelessness and defeat. But God—my God—came to the rescue.

He set me in the midst of the most beautiful, quirky, imperfect, but perfect-for-me church family. He ushered me into the hearts of parents who have loved and embraced me with a love that can only come from the heart of Jesus Himself. He taught me faith—faith that believes even when you can't fully see or understand. He led me to buy a home way bigger than what I needed for myself so that others could be welcomed into the experiential knowledge of Kingdom family as well. Before I was even married, I had spiritual daughters living in every room of this four-bedroom home. At one point, one of them was sleeping in the oversized closet upstairs because I ran out of room, and she needed a place to sleep. Talk about an adventure!

I got married, and my husband was welcomed in with the same blessing and overflow of God's love as I was. He grew to love my parents and my spiritual kids, and they him. He would tell you himself that it has changed him. Now we have embraced being spiritual parents together. The fun, the faith, the testing, the endurance, the joy, and the adventure just continues and multiplies. We are committed to pouring love and truth into the lives of the spiritual kids the Lord brings us. We will continue stewarding their hearts as the treasure they are, teaching them in turn to multiply themselves into the lives of others. Our journey is just beginning.

Truly for all of us, though, our journey is just beginning. Allow the Lord to fully define family in your own heart.

There is no greater treasure in heaven or on earth than God's people. What a joy to be entrusted with the cause of loving them well.

Take the risk, be selfless, have faith, and believe.

May your cup runneth over, and may goodness and mercy follow you all the days of your life.

Prayer

Father, Lord Jesus, Holy Spirit,

As You have modeled family for us, help us to embrace Your heart for Your children. Teach us to walk out life as family. We pray that You would set the solitary in families, and that all who cry out to belong would find their place.

In Jesus' name,

Amen

Testimonies

SAMANTHA'S STORY

When you think of Thanksgiving, you think of a day that involves eating a lot of food, gathering with family and friends and, of course, giving thanks for all that you have. Generally, we give thanks on Thanksgiving and receive gifts on Christmas; however, this year my Christmas came early, and other than salvation, I received the greatest gift I could ask for: a revelation of belonging.

The holidays have never held a special place in my heart, not because I didn't like them, but because they have always brought with them the constant reminders of the past and the lack of family—the lack of belonging. I have been blessed with many amazing people throughout the years who have welcomed me to their table and welcomed me to their family, but inside I have always had a place of deep pain and questions that would play on repeat throughout the holidays. "What is wrong with me? Why don't I deserve my own family? What did I do that was so bad?"

This year on Thanksgiving, I was invited, along with my spiritual family, over to our grandparents' house for Thanksgiving dinner. I love Nana and Granddad very much, and I have always known they loved me. But still, on that day I walked in with the heart of a guest. There was a deeper work the Lord wanted to do in my heart on that day. I was still holding back and full of fear that one day even this family wouldn't want me anymore, that somehow I would ruin all the good that I saw around me. We were all welcomed with open arms, hugs and immediate laughter and conversation. I love these moments more than I can say. After settling in for a moment, I walked into the dining room.

There are no words to fully describe what the Lord did in my heart in that moment. Everything seemed to slow down around me as I looked at the table. It was fully set in beautiful décor with room for many people. I moved closer as I looked around the table, and The Lord drew my eyes to a place setting that said my name. I had a place at the table specifically for me, and I had a nametag to prove it.

In that moment, the Lord took me back to holidays in the past that I had spent crying, longing for family. He took me back to holidays that were filled with chaos, arguing and constant discord, and then He gently reminded me of my prayers in those moments and showed me where I was today. It was as if He was whispering to my heart, "I heard you, baby girl, and I want to redeem every single moment of pain if you will let Me."

As my heart screamed, "Yes!" in that moment, the Lord stamped it with His understanding, security, trust and hope. He filled my heart to overflowing with His love and peace as He gave me a true revelation of what it means to belong, not only as a child of His, but to belong and be loved with a godly love by His family. He showed me my fit and released my heart to be at peace and fully myself in the family that He had placed me in. He took me from "guest" to "family."

I was immediately filled with gratitude and true thankfulness, and even now, I want to cry at the memory. There is something so humbling about the goodness of the Lord. It's beyond my comprehension how the Lord can love each of us so much. He loves us so much that He wants to redeem every single thing that the Enemy has stolen. He loves us so much that He wants to redeem even the tiniest memory of pain. Our God is a good God, He is good Father and He always wants to give us more.

I am so thankful for this amazing spiritual family that the Lord has placed me in. Not that this family replaces my biological family or even my chosen family over the years, but each person is an extra blessing on top of all that the Lord has for me. This family has transformed my heart and my life, and I know the Lord has more. He always has more.

It is true that the Lord sets the solitary in families, and it is true that He gives beauty for ashes. It's true that there is room at the table. At the table there is healing. At the table there is nourishment. At the table there is joy. At the table there is redemption. At the table there is peace. At the table there is hope. At the table there is restoration. At the table there is family; and most of all, at the table there is belonging. Come to the table.

A father of the fatherless, a defender of widows, is God in His holy habitation. God sets the solitary in families; He brings out those who are bound into prosperity; but the rebellious dwell in a dry land (Psalms 68:5-6 NKJV).

> *To console those who mourn in Zion, to give them beauty for ashes, the oil of joy for mourning, the garment of praise for the spirit of heaviness; that they may be called trees of righteousness, the planting of the LORD, that He may be glorified* (Isaiah 61:3 NKJV).

> *He heals the brokenhearted and binds up their wounds* (Psalms 147:3 NKJV).

SHERYL'S STORY

I love my family of origin. I was blessed to have an earthly father and mother who loved and believed in me and taught me to love the Lord. My brother and sister-in-law and I are very close. I have so much fun with my niece and grandnephews that even to this day I am known as the big kid. My extended family has many cousins whom I love dearly. Of course, my family is far from perfect, and we have certainly had our share of trials. But, the one constant is the love that we have for each other. What a gift!

God in His wonderful plan has also richly blessed me with spiritual family. He has given me a spiritual father and mother, who continue to love and encourage me. We first became friends when they asked me to be a part of a Lay Renewal Team when I was in college. When God called them to plant a church in Texas, I didn't know how this would affect our relationship, but we continued to stay in close contact. Right after my mom passed away (my dad had passed away fifteen years earlier), I was visiting with them. We were praying together about their upcoming trip to the Philippines. As we were praying, they began blessing me as their first spiritual daughter. God, at that moment, made it official! This past Christmas, we had a great time, along with the rest of my Texas family—their children, grandchildren, and great grandchildren—affirming and enjoying each other. Although they are in a different state, we talk often, they believe in me, pray for me, speak into my life; and we have a wonderful time when we are together. I am so thankful for my Texas spiritual family!

I also recently had an opportunity to visit with another spiritual father, who was my pastor, high school basketball coach, and teacher. We always share precious memories of when he was my pastor, and the love and unity that our church experienced. At age 87, he still vividly remembers details of our basketball games, especially when we would beat Pat Summit's team. God knit my heart together with him and his family at a very impressionable time in my life. Their love, Godly counsel, and encouragement helped shape and continue to influence who I am today.

Spiritual family is multifaceted for me. About thirty-eight years ago, when I was a teacher, one of my students, asked me to come to her home for dinner. Little did I know that God had another spiritual family—a sister, brother, children, and grandchildren planned for me. My student's mom and I became friends, business partners, and ministry partners. More importantly, we all became spiritual family and have spent almost four decades living life up close and personal together. Be careful who you ask to come to dinner—you never know what God is going to do!

Even though I do not have biological children, God has blessed me with spiritual children. Those children include two of my former students, who are gifts to me. They now serve on our Board and strongly support our ministry. Talk about coming full circle!

I am also thankful to have other spiritual daughters that God has brought into my life through teaching, church, and facilitating HOPE Workshops. I love them all, and I cannot imagine doing life without any of them! I am so blessed!

Our Heavenly Father's love for us is extravagant and limitless. He wants us to deeply experience His love so that we can love those He has put in our lives. So, He gives us spiritual family to love and be loved by in the good times and the hard times. We walk together—encouraging and affirming each other—grounded in His great love for us. I John 3:1 says, *See what great love the Father has lavished on us, that we should be called the children of God.* Spiritual family—belonging—it's our Father's heart for us!

MIKE'S STORY

I came to New Song Christian Fellowship when I was broken and in need of healing, and God has used this church community as a balm for my soul. Not only has He used them to bringing healing to me, but He has used them as a catalyst to raise up and release all that God has placed within me. This spiritual family has included faithful and loving leaders who have been very important in my growth in the Lord, and their encouragement and leadership has been vital to all of my relationships. My wonderful spiritual parents, Pastor Dale Evrist, his wife, Joan, and Pastor Toni Kline, have helped me to see that there is tremendous worth and greatness in all of us, and God desires to draw those things out of us through mentoring, discipleship and coaching in the context of the Body of Christ.

My spiritual dad, Pastor Dale, has shown me the importance of how to truly love the Word of God. Through him I have become a better student of the Word and of the Spirit. Our partnership has also highlighted for me the importance of mutual impartation by not only receiving from Pastor Dale, but having the opportunity to give and release revelation that I receive from the Lord to him. Pastor Dale has helped me develop a listening ear for the voice of God, and for that I am eternally grateful.

My spiritual mom, Pastor Toni, has been a tremendous blessing and gift from the Lord, not just to me but to so many. She has shown me what a faithful follower of Jesus truly looks like. Having her as a spiritual mother has also helped me understand the heart and compassion of God as she expresses His "motherly" love to me in ways I need. She has helped me to see that while God is just, He is also full of mercy and grace, and she draws that mercy towards others out of me.

One of the most important blessings I found in the context of my spiritual family is my wife, Sarah. She is a true treasure and reminder that God's plans are discovered as you embrace life lived in the Body of Christ. She is an amazing mother and woman of God, and I am truly grateful that He placed us in the same spiritual family. She has the heart of a true worshipper, and we are truly blessed not just to have one another but our three precious daughters as well.

In addition to the spiritual mothers and fathers God has given me, He has also given me faith-filled brothers and sisters to walk out this life with. These are they who "stick closer than a brother," and they have been a tremendous strength and support for me and my family.

I have come to learn that, just as God chooses your biological family, He also chooses your spiritual family. It was imperative for me to meet and develop authentic relationships with spiritual parents and brothers and sisters in Christ. I've become the man I am today because of all that has been poured into me through them. I am a better son, a better father, a better husband and a better friend because of the examples set by my spiritual family. They have been essential to my life, and I can't imagine living any other way.

MORGAN'S STORY

Home—a word that can bring up so many feelings—warm feelings, feelings of love and security, or feelings of loneliness, anger, emptiness. Home is where the heart is, people would say. Not for me. Home was a little chaotic, unsettling at times, dysfunctional, a place of mistrust, and a place where I had to grow up a lot faster than a normal kid.

As I was graduating high school in California, I felt the Lord leading me to a huge transition. After hearing about an internship at a church in Nashville, TN, I knew that's where He wanted me to be. I would have never thought I would be living in Nashville 3,000 miles away from "home." I never would have imagined He was leading me towards a healthy marriage and a home of peace and restoration. I would have never thought I would have spiritual parents as role models and brothers and sisters to share life with in church community. Most unexpected of all, I never thought that I would see the promises of the Lord in His Word become so tangibly evident in my life.

Eight years ago, I moved to Nashville; I was broken, bitter, angry, and filled with secrets and pain from my past. I had packed all my stuff into my little old Honda Civic and moved across the country. Little did I know I was about to meet and move in with my spiritual family. After being there for a brief time, I got to know this family, and they just welcomed me so warmly. In the months that followed, they continued to embrace and include me, until eventually they ended up inviting me to be a part of their family.

Soon after, the Lord began to uncover lies I had been believing, and He began to help me break down my emotional walls. He taught me to walk in forgiveness, He led me to let go of expectations, and I began to allow God and my spiritual family access to parts of my heart that were completely shut off until then.

It wasn't an easy process AT ALL. I can remember at one point feeling like I was being targeted by the Enemy on every side. I wanted to give up. Was this worth it? Did I really need to go through all this to walk with Christ? I kept asking myself these questions, but I didn't give up. I couldn't. Some nights I would lay awake praying, listening to worship music and rebuking the lies of the Enemy in order to receive God's truth. I came to understand that sometimes the deepest healing and freedom the Lord wants to bring won't come without a fight, and I mean a fight! My spiritual family didn't give up. My leaders didn't give up. They encouraged me, believed in me, challenged me and stood with me. I needed that, especially coming from a history where family danced in and out of my life at their convenience. They didn't stick around when things were hard. The Lord was rebuilding my trust by showing me He was with me through it all, and so was my spiritual family.

Finally, I was at home. I had a place I could run to, and it was safe—a place full of laughter and joy, a place of peace and unity. It was always there, but it took me walking through a process of healing to allow myself to accept it and to live securely in my identity as a daughter. Even the day I received a call that my grandpa passed away, the man who had been a father to me most of my life, I knew that I wasn't without a father.

When my wedding day came over a year later, as I walked down the aisle with my spiritual dad, I thought back to all the moments of God's redemption in my life, including every moment that led up to that day! I was about to marry a man I had waited for, prayed for, and knew that I was ready for. God gave me great spiritual parents as role models, which prepared me to embark on this new adventure as a wife and a mother someday. I NEVER thought those words would ever come out of my mouth, much less that I would think such things. The Lord never leaves us nor forsakes us; He always knows what we need before we do! He sets the solitary in families!

TAMARA'S STORY

It was Christmas eve, and we had just gotten home from our church's Christmas Eve service and had changed into our cozies. I watched my spiritual mom light up with excitement the moment her spiritual parents walked in the door. After they entered, my spiritual grandparents made sure each person in the house was acknowledged and loved on. The friendly banter started, as was the norm, and everyone laughed and had a great time over dinner. This was Christmas Eve with the grandparents.

I thought about how many times throughout the year I had watched moments like these unfold. I watched my spiritual mom, the perfect hostess in my opinion, and was proud to call her mine. She had taught me countless things: how to cook and host, what it meant to budget and plan ahead, how to relate to others with compassion and love, and most of all she taught me to celebrate and honor, and to appreciate each moment with family and truly live in the moment.

This night was no different as I watched her lavish love on her parents. No one could deny that she adored them. She was the one who helped me understand God's design for my heart to have permission to love and be loved to the fullest—the very reason I was in this home on Christmas Eve. She knew firsthand the joy of spiritual family and wanted to make sure that her spiritual daughters experienced the fullness of that joy.

Once dinner was complete, it was time to move the party into the living room, where the fireplace was aglow and Christmas music was softly playing.

We moved on to dessert, hot cocoa, and gift-giving. Traditions were being formed right in front of me. As I sat there, I thought about the year and all that I experienced with them: birthday celebrations, vacations, long nights playing games, grieving together, laughing together, and fighting alongside one another for every promise of the Lord to come to pass. I had seen the victories and the sorrows firsthand, and my heart was overwhelmed with the love of the Lord for each one of them.

This Christmas meant so much more to me than any other Christmas before. It was a picture of why Christ came. Redemption. Love. Peace. Good will. This Christmas Eve, I was experiencing all of these things in the midst of seeing the redemption of holidays and family. I felt the peace of belonging (being fully known and fully loved) and the joy of celebrating each other. We all knew it wasn't about the gifts. It was about Jesus. It was about family. It was the fulfillment of the promise of God to make all things new.

In that moment of gifting-giving, laughter, and peace, I knew that I was established firmly in family. No performance needed, and no need to hide. I was experiencing the purity of family the way the heart of God the Father designed all of us to experience. This was the fruit of trusting the Lord for a new perspective. Disappointment from past holidays faded as the Lord gently reminded me that He will never fail to redeem every broken piece of our lives if we are willing to receive Him.

Growing up, we never spent holidays with family. I always wondered what it would be like to spend holidays, summers, vacations, or just any time with our grandparents'. Even though they lived 10 minutes away, we only saw them a couple of times a year. I remember one Christmas driving past our grandparents house and seeing our cousins playing with our grandparents. It wasn't until I was older that I realized just how much I had wanted to experience those things. My friends would talk about the memories of spending time with their grandparents or aunts and uncles, and I longed for that; it just was never option. I resolved that when I had kids one day, they wouldn't have to live with that same longing. But I never imagined it would change for me.

Spiritual family was a concept that scared and baffled me all at the same time. My sense of loyalty made me concerned that my biological family would see it as replacing them. My fear of being rejected made me want to deny it altogether. But slowly I began to learn the heart of the Lord: He designed family, and He longs for each one of us to be in one where we are safe and "known" and can experience His love. Jesus is the one who established spiritual family while He was on the cross (John 19:26,27).

He made a point to make sure that family was firmly established for His mother and His beloved disciple, John. His mother had other sons. It wasn't like she needed a son. But there was a perfect fit in the Spirit that caused them to walk in the intimacy of mother and son. This is the very heart of God.

When this concept was first taught to me by my spiritual mom, I was surprised. I had been taught that there should never be anyone other than my biological parents, who could be a mom or dad to me, and that to consider others as "family" was wrong and dishonoring. It took me a while to grasp the concept of spiritual family, but once I did, having spiritual parents suddenly seemed completely logical. The Lord wanted to give the fullness of His heart to me through spiritual family. What my biological family couldn't provide, the Lord provided through my spiritual parents and grandparents. Remarkably, in the midst of it all, I am able to love my biological family even more than before without any shred of resentment for the things I didn't receive growing up. By stepping out in faith in this area, I have been given more than I could ever hope or imagine. My heart is full and grateful.

About the Authors

Rachel Cordero

Rachel is a passionate follower of Jesus Christ. Her commitment to being a mouthpiece for the Lord comes from her miraculous story of God's redeeming love. Born and raised in Northern California, she has more than 15 years of ministry experience from working with youth, young adults, and women in the areas of counseling, grief recovery, and trauma. She has a deep passion to write on these topics and to help equip the Church at large to minister effectively to these issues. Rachel obtained a B.A. in Biblical Counseling from Trinity Seminary and has an M.A. in Counseling from Liberty University. She and her husband, Leon, live in Spring Hill, TN with a house full of spiritual daughters and two teacup Yorkie's named Bailey and Bella.

Toni Kline

For more than 25 years as a Counselor and Pastor, Toni Kline has had a passion for seeing the next generation discipled, mentored, and coached unto being raised up and released as mature spiritual sons and daughters in the Lord. Her love for the Lord and for His Word are contagious, and as a gifted teacher and communicator, she is a blessing to many. She received her B.S. from Lee University in Psychology and her M.A. in Counseling from Liberty University. She serves as an Associate Pastor at New Song Christian Fellowship and has worked with young adults for the past 15 years. She lives in Franklin, TN with her husband, Kevin, and they enjoy having his parents as a part of their ever-changing household.

Notes

Bible Gateway. *https://www.Biblegateway.com/resources/commentaries/IVP-NT/John/Jesus-Is-Crucified.* n.d. Commentary. 15 6 2015.

Blue Letter Bible. *http://www.blueletterBible.org/search/Dictionary/viewTopic.cfm?topic=VT0000994.* n.d. Dictionary. 15 6 2015.

Cloud, Dr. Henry and Dr. John Townsend. *Boundaries.* Grand Rapids MI: Zondervan, 1992.

Hayford, Jack. *The Spirit Filled Life Bible.* Nashville, TN: Thomas Nelson, 2002. Book.

Mirriam-Webster. *http://www.merriam-webster.com/dictionary/family.* 15 June 2015.

The Boxtrolls. Dir. Anthony Stacchi Graham Annable. Perf. Ben Kingsley. 2014. DVD.

The Little Mermaid. Dir. John Musker Ron Clements. Perf. Walt Disney. 1989. DVD.

[i] (Disney)
[ii] (Mirriam-Webster)
[iii] (Blue Letter Bible)
[iv] (Bible Gateway)

Made in the USA
Charleston, SC
01 February 2017